THE KOWLOON KID

A HONG KONG CHILDHOOD

THE KOWLOON KID

A HONG KONG CHILDHOOD

PHIL BROWN

MELBOURNE, AUSTRALIA
www.transitlounge.com.au

First published 2019
Transit Lounge Publishing

Cover and book design: Peter Lo
Author image: David Kelly

Printed in Australia by McPherson's Printing Group

A cataloguing-entry is available from the
National Library of Australia: trove.nla.gov.au
ISBN: 978-1-925760-36-1

For my parents
Edward John Brown and Janet McLaren Brown
And my grandfather, Lord Roberts Brown

'Squeezed between giant antagonists crunching huge bones of contention, Hong Kong has achieved within its own narrow territories a co-existence which is baffling, infuriating, incomprehensible, and works splendidly – on borrowed time in a borrowed place.'

Han Suyin, *Hong Kong's Ten Year Miracle, Life* magazine

'Hong Kong is an astounding epilogue of Empire.'

Jan Morris, *Hong Kong*

'You can leave Hong Kong, but it will never leave you.'

Nury Vittachi, *Hong Kong: The City of Dreams*

CONTENTS

CHAPTER 1

IN THE LOBBY

The lobby of The Peninsula Hong Kong is always lovely but it's particularly romantic around dusk.

The hotel's High Tea crowd dissipates in the late afternoon, leaving only a tinkling piano as a reminder of its genteel mayhem. On this particular evening one or two High Tea takers remained in a corner lingering over their tiered- sandwich-and-cake trays, sipping what must be cold tea by now, basking in the sumptuous splendour … perhaps lingering longer than they were supposed to. The *maître d'* hovers nearby and a trickle of *tai tais* in designer dresses usher in the dawning of the cocktail hour. The sun has gone, darkness is falling and the lights from the passing traffic on Salisbury Road outside are reflected in a damp sheen created by light rainfall.

In the lobby a subtle, golden-hued gloaming is created by the gilt rococo splendour of the surrounds. The almost ethereal light softens everything. Bellboys swing open the heavy glass doors with their gold handles so that an elderly man, alighting from a green Rolls-Royce, can make his way between the attendant stone carved lions, through the doors and on towards reception. So rich he can barely walk, clad in crumpled leisurewear, the gentleman shuffles past me followed by two bellboys laden with his matching Louis Vuitton luggage.

There I stood, a tad wobbly, taking in this scene after coming down from my De Luxe Harbour View Suite on the 21st floor for some respite from the messy, albeit luxurious bed where I had spent the last few days tossing and turning with an unidentified ague.

I was, I declared with some certainty, quite possibly dying.

"Again?" my wife asked. It's the sort of terse response given by someone tiring of a hypochondriac's litany of woes. Sandra suggested a De Luxe Harbour View Suite at The Peninsula Hong Kong was not the worst place to perish and I certainly couldn't argue with that. After that exchange I had reclined again and in my mind's eye saw Jeremy Irons expiring on the Kowloon waterfront in the film *Chinese Box*. Hong Kong's harbour was the last thing he saw and I had lain abed, wracked with fever, thinking it might be the same for me. That wouldn't be so bad though because it was, after all, a view of heaven as far as I was concerned.

Between torrid naps I would sit up and watch the Star ferries track back and forth, see the cruise ships come and go, and note something that made the scene quite different from the view I recalled from childhood. There in the midst of the harbour was a Chinese warship where once there would have been a British vessel. I had grown up in Hong Kong in the 1960s when it was a British Crown colony and found the new reality a tad disconcerting.

Once upon a time the ships and ferries and pleasure boats would have jostled with sampans and noble junks. There was still a smattering of sampans yet only a couple of junks still plied the harbour, transporting tourists on pleasure cruises. They seemed to bob like children's toys in a bath as they circled Victoria Harbour far below.

Before I had fallen ill a ride on one of these junks had been arranged for us. The boat was wistfully named the *Duk Ling*. The planned voyage followed a rather traumatic lunch at another hotel nearby where they had insisted on hosting us for a banquet, an excruciating three-hour affair in a swish dining room. Our son Hamish, who was just eight at the time, had attended to his lunch in the same way Jackson Pollock painted and turned the immaculate tablecloth into his own work of art using the medium of soy sauce. He had managed to fling rice to the four corners of the room while we winced and looked at our watches as the dishes kept coming. I was so full I was tempted to ask for a bucket but to save face I just kept eating.

After lunch and feeling some relief to be out in the open again, we had wandered several hundred metres to the *Duk Ling*'s embarkation point, clutching our tickets like lottery winners. The wharf is next to the Star ferry terminal and from there we watched the antique vessel approach, gorgeously exotic with its twin serrated sails and insistent poop deck. The junk has always been a symbol of the Orient for me and in my Hong Kong childhood they were fixtures in the waters off every beach we visited. Picture-postcard scenes with junks sailing past, almost on cue, are etched in my memory, in our family album and, as it happens, on the walls of our house in Brisbane. We have two of those junk paintings that every tourist to Hong Kong should procure, heavy impasto harbour scenes with a strident junk in the centre of it all.

Taken with the exotic otherness of the idea, I had long been determined to ride the green, glassy waters of the Harbour on the *Duk Ling* but had never got around to it on any of my many previous visits back to Hong Kong. I wanted to imagine myself living back in the days when princes and pirates journeyed by this mode of transport.

When the *Duk Ling* finally arrived, rocking violently back and forth in the wake of a nearby ferry, we watched it with more than a little trepidation. Soon it berthed and began to disgorge passengers, people white as sheets in various stages of torment, wracked by seasickness. They staggered past us like walking wounded or extras from a zombie movie, one woman so ill she had to be carried off. And as they hauled her up the gangplank and past us I saw a look of horror on her face that reminded me of that Wilfred Owen poem *Dulce et Decorum Est* which chronicles the aftermath of a mustard-gas attack in the trenches of World War I. Owen described one victim as having a face '*like a devil's sick of sin*'. That was her to a T.

Her limp figure then convulsed and she proceeded to vomit down the front of her soiled dress before slumping into exhausted unconsciousness as they lay her gently on the concrete, using her handbag as a pillow.

I had surrendered my tickets to the sailor attending the gangplank directly after witnessing that display. When he took them from me and gestured for us to come aboard I waved him away and we fled, retreating back across Salisbury Road to the safety of the hotel. As we did I shouted "*Faai di laa*!" ("Hurry up!") in Cantonese.

"It's much better to just watch it from up here," I said later back in the room as I sat sipping tea and watching the *Duk Ling* circle the harbour.

I had been feeling a little indisposed, as it happened, after our banquet and thought it might have been from overeating. But that mild feeling of indisposition was a mere precursor. The following day I was struck down with the fever that had confined me to my luxury suite for several days now. Between witnessing a never-ending story unfolding on the waters below I watched cheesy old movies and ordered tea and soup, all I could manage under the circumstances. The rest of the time I spent swooning and moaning, which drove my wife and son from the room.

I had to get over the fever before I could fly home. Bird flu was still a threat and the sensors at the airport would pick up my temperature if I presented while still in the grip of fever. So I had to bring my temperature down somehow.

If my exact malady was unclear, how I came by it wasn't. I could trace its provenance back to the very moment of contamination, an episode that occurred walking down Salisbury Road the day after we had arrived in Hong Kong on this latest voyage into my past. I have spent my entire adult life trying to conjure up my colonial glory days like some spiritualist striving to communicate with the other side.

This trip was my son Hamish's first, and on our way in from the airport he had noted that Hong Kong (an anglicised version of *Heung Gong*, meaning Fragrant Harbour) had its own peculiar pong, to which I had responded: "Smellcome to Hong Kong", one of my lamer dad jokes.

The next day I was walking with my boy along Salisbury Road towards the ferry terminal when a passing pedestrian sneezed in my face. There was no attempt at shielding others from the nasal ejaculation, no modesty or consideration involved at all, just a full-bodied spray. I knew at that moment, as the droplets hit my epidermis, that I was doomed.

So what was it, this tropical fever that gripped me like some cholera-stricken character in a tale of old Cathay? If it was, on the other hand, bird flu I could pinpoint exactly when and where I caught it and hopefully that might help the authorities, who would no doubt embark on an investigation using CCTV footage to identify the carrier.

After the onset I had checked my temperature with the thermometer we had in our bathroom bag and then approached my PR contact at the hotel to ask – sounding like someone in an old *Carry On* movie – if there was a doctor in the house. No. Not in-house, I was told, however there was one in the neighbourhood. She promised to make an appointment and call me straight back. Within minutes the phone rang and I was told someone would come to the room shortly to escort me there.

When the doorbell rang Sandra opened it to find a delegation – two young women and a security man in a suit. I knew he was a security man by the wire leading to the earpiece he tapped as we approached the lift. He muttered something in Cantonese as the lift doors closed and I assumed he was talking to someone sitting in front of a bank of screens in a room somewhere, *reporting in* that the package had been picked up and was on its way to the delivery point.

The three of them escorted me through the luxury shopping arcade that borders the lobby and out into the street, the two young women waving me off at the kerb as the security man ushered me across the road. It was but a short walk to our destination, a building nearby, and we went up a few floors in a small lift. Then I was led into a small frigid waiting room. Air conditioning in Hong Kong is often Arctic but this was more Antarctic and we were buffeted by something more akin to a katabatic wind than a breeze.

I waited for the doctor who soon appeared wearing one of those white coats over his suit that medicos here don't bother with any more. It was a statement – *I'm a doctor*. A stethoscope hung from his neck just in case there was any question still lingering as to his identity.

I followed him into his office while the security man gestured that he would wait outside, touching his earpiece again as if to check that it was still on. He then said, in a low voice, something in Cantonese that may have indicated the eagle had landed.

The doctor sat me on a bench and made me stick out my tongue. He felt my glands, took my temperature and looked knowingly at the thermometer.

"I think I may have bird flu," I said without irony.

He ignored me and continued his examination: listening to my heart, checking my blood pressure and then taking my temperature again as if to confirm his worst suspicions.

"No flu, juss fever," he said. "Maybe infection. I give antibiotic. You not allergic?"

"No," I said. "But I have to fly back to Australia in a few days and I'm worried about the sensors at the airport picking me up." He looked at me quizzically.

"Too hot," I said, touching my forehead. He nodded knowingly.

"Not problem," he said. "Take tablet, two days will be OK fly. Keep rest, lot of water."

He wrote a prescription and I went back out to pay his receptionist who was so cold she had goose bumps on her arms. The security man escorted me to a nearby pharmacy where I had the prescription filled and purchased some more paracetamol.

"I told you it wasn't bird flu," Sandra said when I got back to the room. I took the first dose of the antibiotic, poured myself a glass of chilled water, got back into bed and proceeded to watch *Twister* which, despite the fact that I love it, may just be one of the silliest movies ever made.

Over the next day or so Sandra and Hamish came and went while I rarely ventured from the room until, on this particular evening, as I watched the evening lights come on across the harbour, I decided to walk downstairs to the lobby by myself to stretch my legs.

And there I stood in the place that has always felt like my spiritual home, the lobby of The Pen, as we Hong Kongers call it. In the 1960s this was the centre of our social life but my family have actually been regulars since the late 1930s when my grandfather brought his family and his construction company to Hong Kong as he fled south from Shanghai, escaping the invading Japanese army. In those days of Empire, there were tea dances and swish dinners and I sometimes imagine him dreaming of this lobby as he was nearly starved to death in the prisoner-of-war camp at Stanley where he spent most of World War II on that peninsula near where the famous Stanley Market is today.

The Peninsula Hong Kong, built in 1928, was known as

the best hotel east of Suez. When the Japanese took control of Hong Kong in 1941 they made it their headquarters and renamed it The Toa (East Asia) hotel. The British officially surrendered in a room at the hotel.

When in turn the Japanese eventually surrendered (on August 30, 1945) the hotel regained its place as the hub of Kowloon society life and my grandfather, grandmother, their four sons and three daughters were all regulars there – as we were later, in the Swinging Sixties. The fact that I regard it as my spiritual home sounds like an affectation. The idea of a hotel lobby as a kind of New Jerusalem seems a little unreal, I know, but for me it's true.

It has always been a special place for me, a touchstone, and I return recurrently with Nietzschean repetition, searching for something I will never quite find again. Something that may never have existed in the first place except in my imagination.

I'm part of a diaspora of old Hong Kongers, former colonials wandering the earth with memories of their Hong Kong childhoods shadowing them like the Ghost of Christmas Past. For all the times we leave we have never *really* left and still think of Hong Kong as home. We have Facebook pages now where we share photos of the lost world of childhood and tell stories about them, stories that sound like something by W. Somerset Maugham.

Old Hong Kongers of all nationalities can be found in the far-flung corners of the planet. One of my closest friends from childhood, a garrulous Englishman by the name of Mark Reeve, came to visit us in Australia some years ago while on a world tour catching up with old schoolfriends from Hong Kong days. He visited several continents and was never without a bed offered by some old pal who, like all of us, enjoyed nothing more than staying up into the wee hours reminiscing about the good old dying days of that colony of Empire upon which, once upon a very good time, the sun never set.

I'm one of these bores who can never quite relate to the world except through the lens of Hong Kong … a confused individual whose Australianness is laced with vestiges of my very British-colonial salad days.

In my dreams, and even in my waking hours, I sometimes find myself in a reverie, walking the Kowloon streets again, navigating its bustling sidewalks and laneways, hailing the occasional rickshaw, being ferried to school by the driver, having my bath drawn for me by the domestic servant – our amah – on cool winter evenings. Is it wrong to yearn for that life of privilege at a time when the idea of Empire seems such a mistake?

Still I yearn for a world ruled by a Governor in a white hat adorned with ostrich feathers, for the old Kowloon where Sikh guards with shotguns guarded the banks, for a time when the noonday gun that Noël Coward wrote about in his song *Mad Dogs and Englishmen* was fired as the British flag fluttered in the breeze while Mao Tse-tung's Cultural Revolution ravaged China, just across the border.

Amid so much change in Hong Kong the lobby of The Pen is a constant and the hotel remains a symbol and a monument to the past, a portal for people like me to do some time-travelling.

Yes, a new tower juts above the hotel now, but the colonial splendour remains and the lobby is still a warm and welcoming place where you find an attendant in the loo who will smile and hand you soap and a towel despite your embarrassment, in a place when you would rather be left alone to attend to your business. I usually accept the proffered help and then press a low denomination of banknote into the attendant's palm as I leave, telling myself that I am assisting the local economy.

Standing in the foyer on this particular evening, mind foggy from the fever, I sought a table, slumped into a chair and ordered a cup of jasmine tea. Guiltily I explained that I was a guest (in case there was some question about that, looking crumpled as I did and in case there was disappointment that a cup of tea was all I wanted).

After the hubbub of High Tea, when the queue goes out the door and snakes into the shopping arcade, it's nice to enjoy the lobby's splendour in relative calm … to sit and watch people come and go as the hotel's fleet of Rollers disgorge their payloads.

As I sat there, my fever still present yet possibly subsiding, I closed my eyes, then opened them again and imagined, in that ambient, glamorous gloom, the ghosts of the past crowding around me.

It was odd. There was the lobby as it once was, as intact as a scene from a movie I could watch in my own head, a movie starring … my father, Edward John Brown … Ted, who came here every day from his office nearby to do business. Dad's last office in Hong Kong, in the 1960s, was rather handily in Hankow Rd, virtually next door.

He'd been coming here since he was a boy. Long dead, taken at 55 with a little help from a certain Scotch whisky, I could see him now, his ebullience obvious from a distance – the gleaming white smile, ubiquitous white sliver of pocket square sticking out of his tailored suit-jacket pocket, his heavy gold ring glinting from across the room.

The Pen was like our living room, a home away from home as well as my old man's unofficial office. Often we would come in and join him here on Saturday mornings after the rigours of our activities at the YMCA, which was, and still is, just across the road. We would order Coke floats and eat ice cream with long parfait spoons. My parents would mingle with friends at nearby tables while helpful boys (the waiters were always "boys" regardless of age) would cater to our every whim.

Some had been denizens of that foyer since the post-war years, people like my father's friend, a Scotsman called John Prosser-Inglis who was better known as Jock. He arrived in Hong Kong after World War II and established himself as one of the regulars in the lobby at The Pen with his own table. Some regulars had their own name plaque on their tables. He carried out all his business in that lobby. The parade of celebrities was never-ending. Kings, queens and film stars could often be spotted here.

If you sat in the foyer long enough you would see someone famous. I keenly remember one day my father came home, bearing autographs, as he often did, for me and my brother and sister. This time his booty consisted of scribbled names we couldn't quite discern but he pointed out who they were – one was from the American actor Steve McQueen, the other from Hollywood director Robert Wise. They were in Hong Kong at the time filming *The Sand Pebbles*, a film about China in the warlord years of the 1920s and my father, never a shy man, spotted McQueen, a huge star at the time, made a beeline for him and felt comfortable enough to do that because, well, they were sitting in his field office after all. Apparently my father had fronted them by saying, "G'day Steve, I'm Ted Brown from Australia. Let me buy you a drink."

He had sat and chatted to them for a while, reporting to us that McQueen was a terrific bloke. My mother seemed disappointed she hadn't been with him.

That was my father's adopted Australian egalitarianism at work. The funny thing was, my father was actually British. Growing up I never once heard him identify himself as an Englishman though he was born in London and raised in colonial Hong Kong. It was his years in Australia during World War II, when he served in the AIF, that turned him into an Australian. To Steve McQueen he was just another friendly Aussie and that's how he thought of himself.

I thought of my father, now remembered as a character in a story written long ago. I peered into the rich gloom and imagined him and the other businessmen drinking, always too early in the day, swilling the ice around in their glasses, smug as any colonial could be. There were businessmen and travellers, China hands or China watchers as they used to call the old journos who drank there as they faded away far from home. One such was the Australian Richard Hughes whose book *Borrowed Place, Borrowed Time: Hong Kong and Its Many Faces* was something of a wake-up call. Was it really possible – as he was suggesting half a century ago – that Hong Kong would one day return to what was known as Red China? We shuddered at the idea as the bodies from executions in the Cultural Revolution floated down the Pearl Delta and into Hong Kong harbour. This was the Cold War era and conflict raged in Vietnam too. Some of those characters who gathered in The Pen were obviously spies, an idea that tantalised me as a boy and still does. Hughes, who had covered the North African campaign of World War II as well as the Korean and Vietnam wars, was considered a British spy and by some to be a double agent.

I peered into the gloom again and saw the bellboys rushing around with those little blackboards they used to grasp, that had bicycle bells attached. As they cut past the tables you could see a name scrawled in chalk. There was an important telephone call, quite possibly a fake.

My dad reckoned half the businessmen who drank there would page themselves to feign a sense of importance, pressing coins into a bellboy's hand as they arranged the deception out of sight in a hallway off the lobby.

I could see all this. Then the waiter brought the bill and it evaporated. I felt like Coleridge whose reverie had been disturbed by an insurance salesman knocking on his door, which was why he never finished his poem about Xanadu.

My poetic vision vanished too. I signed the chit and then my mobile rang.

"Where are you? my wife asked.

"I'm still down in the lobby," I said. "I'm having a cup of jasmine tea."

"Well, come back up and have a shower and we'll order some room service," she said. She and my son had been out much of the afternoon shopping at Harbour City, a mall where I have often found myself trapped, unable to find an exit.

I finished my tea and wandered past reception, nodding to the girls with exquisitely coiffed hair behind the desk, guessing that they realised I wasn't as rich as the old man who had passed by earlier. Should I explain to them that I was just some journalist with a liquidity problem searching for his long-lost childhood? Best not.

I went back upstairs, ordered some soup, and later we watched another old movie with the lights on low. I had one eye on the screen and the other on the harbour and the neon wonderland of Hong Kong's CBD across the water. A cruise ship, lit up like a Christmas tree, barged past heading for the Ocean Terminal.

Later, mist rolled in across the water and I pulled the curtains to, leaving them only slightly apart so I could drift off to sleep with some vestige of a harbour view, the lights now blurring with the fog. Eventually I was out to it, beads of sweat pearling on my brow as the fever began to break. And I dreamt of old Hong Kong.

CHAPTER 2

THE DEATH OF MOUSIE TUNG

In early 1963 we moved … suddenly, or so it seemed … to Hong Kong. My father had disappeared from our house in the suburb of Lorn in the Hunter Valley town of Maitland, New South Wales. A week or so later my mother got a call and that was it. She was to pack up and fly to Hong Kong. Straight away. My father was an impetuous man.

I had just settled into a tiny primary school called Nillo, which was in the suburb where we lived, and I think I was happy enough there. There's a photo of me adorning a Nativity scene with a few other kids. I'm tying tinsel to a manger. I'm always drawn to that photo because in it I look quite serene. I have never again achieved the same modicum of serenity, except perhaps by artificial means.

My mother, Janet (mostly known as Jan) was, I think, hoping we would settle down in Maitland, for a few years at least, after a peripatetic life following the fortunes and jobs of my father's family construction company, the rather unimaginatively titled Brown's Constructions.

Mum wanted some security, possibly because her childhood

had been disrupted. Her father Alfred McLaren Scott was a country bank manager in Queensland. She was born in Bundaberg when her father was managing the bank at Childers, a sugar town that was little more than a village. Later they lived in North Queensland, and then she and her sister Meg became boarders at Brisbane Girls Grammar School while my grandfather moved from bank to bank. The story goes that my maternal grandmother, who was apparently a bit of a snob and liked her sherry a bit too much, refused to go to one of his postings and my grandfather was punished by being sent to Woodenbong, a small timber town just across the NSW border in a land that time forgot. My mum had left school and she went too, worked in her dad's bank and promptly had a nervous breakdown, suffering and suffocating in the isolation. I have never been to Woodenbong and it's not exactly on my bucket list.

She must have been sick of moving around yet she was in for more of it when she met my father.

Brown's Constructions involved my dad, Ted; his brothers Cyril, Bob and, increasingly less, Harold, an unreliable alcoholic; and their brother-in-law, another ex-Hong Konger, an Englishman by the name of John Wheeler. Plus my grandfather Bob, who thought he was in charge. I gather the company hierarchy was fracturing somewhat by the time we came to settle in Maitland for the second time – and if you had met my family you'd know why.

Brown's Constructions was the antipodean iteration of my Grandad Bob's Asian business China Construction Co., a company he'd run in China and Hong Kong before World War II and again in the colony afterwards. He moved the company (renaming it in the process) and the family to Australia in the early 1950s to escape the Red Peril (the threat of communism when China was declared the People's Republic in 1949) and they worked all over the country building bridges and engaging in major civil engineering projects. Foundation work was their speciality. There were expectations early on that I would one day follow in my father's footsteps ... that was never going to happen. The mysteries of bore piling and coffer dams held no allure for me and, anyway, my maths was always appalling.

Dad built a couple of bridges in Maitland, one of them the Belmore Bridge which straddles the Hunter River in the middle of town. That bridge was washed away in the great flood of 1955, which sounds a bit biblical and it really was. If you've ever seen Phillip Noyce's seminal 1978 Australian film *Newsfront* you may recall a scene featuring those floods with a cine-camera crew navigating the main street in a rowboat.

Mum was working in the bank at Maitland at the time when Brown's Constructions was engaged to rebuild the Belmore Bridge. My parents met and got married pretty soon afterwards, in December 1955. Their wedding was at Lindfield in Sydney because that was the Brown family seat. For their honeymoon they flew to Singapore, where they stayed at the famous Raffles Hotel, and then went on to Hong Kong where they stayed – of course – at The Peninsula. They came back and at first settled in Maitland where my father built a second bridge on the edge of town. Being a long bridge across a floodplain, it was called, appropriately enough, The Long Bridge. There was obviously an imagination deficiency in Maitland back then.

Between our times in Maitland there was a stint in Devonport, Tasmania, where the company was responsible for the foundations of the wharf for the *Princess of Tasmania* ferry. My mother's main memory of that time was that it was so cold my nappies used to freeze on the line. Hopefully she thawed them out before putting them on me. Later we moved to Albury where my sister was born and we kept moving, from job to job, settling briefly in Sydney, in a house on a hill at Narrabeen, where my brother Stephen first saw the light of day.

Then it was back to Maitland for our second stretch in what should technically count as my hometown. It never completely feels like my hometown although I do have a nostalgic fondness for the place and we make a pilgrimage there every few years. That second time around in Maitland the company had the job of refurbishing the Belmore Bridge after another minor flood. They called my father 'Floody Brown' because half the bridges he built had been affected by floods one way or another.

While I'm sure Mum thought we might have been settling down there, my father had long been hankering to go back to Hong Kong. He was ambitious in his way and wanted to emulate Grandad Bob, "the old man", and when he heard there was a building boom in Hong Kong – there always seems to be one and that has never changed – he flew off to investigate. I'm not sure if my mother realised how advanced his plans were. Looking back, I realise he must have already made some because we had a mysterious Chinese visitor some months before that, the son of my father's future business partner – a spiv we only ever knew as Tang. The Tangs were one of the most powerful clans in Hong Kong and, hell, they'd even once had a dynasty named after them. I remember we took Tang's son to the beach and I was surprised that he spoke English.

I was quite happy at Nillo School, of which I have only fleeting memories. Besides helping put the finishing touches on the Nativity scene I recall great excitement when a small circus troupe came to the school with performing goats. We were all amused because the goats pooped all over the playground.

I can recall the taste of curdled milk. At Australian primary schools they used to force you to drink a small bottle of milk every day, and often the crates would have been sitting in the sun too long by the time we got to them. I also remember the smell of cream buns delivered to the school in a large wooden tray from a local bakery.

Our family home, which my father had just bought, had a small backyard which was largely taken up by a patch of corn. There's a photo of my paternal grandmother, who used to wear Dame Edna glasses, standing in that corn patch holding my brother, who was just a baby at the time. A gaggle of girls lived across the road, several sisters who taught me how to ride a bike. Some boys might have baulked at that but I was kind of sweet on them so I had no problem with it.

We might have had a good life in Maitland because it was a nice town and still is. When people ask me where I'm from I always start with Maitland and then, to make it seem more relevant, I reel off the names of significant people who were also born in the town or its environs – bushranger Ben Hall, legendary boxer Les Darcy, actor Ruth Cracknell, the great thespian John Bell, playwright Nick Enright, theatre director David Berthold … the list goes on.

Sometimes I wonder how things might have been had we stayed in that pleasant and historic town. Futile speculation: it wasn't to be.

All of a sudden we were whisked away one day by Qantas V-Jet (the V stood for *vannus*, Latin for 'fan'), a Boeing 707, that enduring symbol of the jet-set age. One minute I was rustling around in the corn patch out back of the house in Maitland, next I knew I was in an aircraft cabin high above the world with bright sunlight streaming in on a clear blue Australian autumn day.

I was soon commandeered by a friendly hostess and talked into helping hand around a basket of Minties to fellow passengers. It was all a bit of an adventure. Clearly visible out the cabin window below were the archipelago, volcanoes and reefs of The Philippines as we flew into a Northern Hemisphere spring. In adult life I've always been an anxious airline passenger, to say the least. I pull the shade down over the cabin window and concentrate on watching movies to distract from what seems to me the utter precariousness of air travel. But then I was six and excited to be going to Hong Kong, although I really had no concept of the place.

"Is it anything like Maitland?" I asked my mum, to which she shook her head and looked quite emphatic.

At Kai Tak International Airport – one of the world's most exhilarating landings, on that famous finger of concrete runway that jutted into Kowloon Bay – we were met by my dad and a driver who took us to our temporary home in St George's Court tower block, an eyrie for expats on a hill at the top of Kadoorie Avenue in Ho Man Tin, mid-Kowloon. Kadoorie Ave. is named after the enterprising Kadoorie family, Jews originally from Baghdad who moved to the Far East to make their fortune. They founded Hong Kong and Shanghai Hotels and built The Peninsula, bless them.

At St George's Court we lived in what is known as a 'leave flat', a home vacated temporarily by the regular inhabitants, stuffy English folk according to my father. They had gone home for several months on a long break that meant they would miss Hong Kong's humid summer, considered by many to be intolerable and incompatible with proper civilised life.

In this furnished and spacious flat my father seemed at home. And it came with an amah, a domestic servant. All expats in this exotic colony had employed women who often had come from China to seek a new life in Hong Kong.

We inherited our amah with the flat. She was a rather terrifying woman called Ah Chan. My mother was very uncomfortable with the idea of having another woman in the house, one who thought she was actually in charge even though she called my parents "Master" and "Missy" with what sounded a little like grudging respect.

Ah Chan resented us, I'm sure she did. I reckon she wanted the flat to herself in the boss's absence Instead, here were these coarse Australian interlopers with their three bothersome children – me, my sister Jane and my little brother Stephen. I can clearly remember that she wore a persistent scowl during the months we lived there preparing for our future life in Hong Kong. My mother said she couldn't wait to move and hire her own amah, so for her St George's Court meant long months spent in a power struggle with Ah Chan.

Little did my mother know that Ah Chan was getting her own back in a cunning fashion, even as she bowed and scraped and pretended to be servile.

We ordered our groceries from a supplier known in colonial parlance as a comprador, a kind of glorified grocer who obtained things for us. This bloke had a shop and office on Cameron Road in Tsim Sha Tsui, downtown Kowloon. He arranged to have supplies delivered to the flat.

Ah Chan took charge of this. Before Mum died I mined her memory about this and she told me that Ah Chan had spent those months scamming us, fiddling the shopping list, over-ordering and then keeping the excess booty in her cramped room beyond the kitchen which was a forbidden zone to us.

My mother ventured in there once when Ah Chan had gone to the local market, acting on suspicions that this amah was up to no good. There she found shelves groaning with cans of food and other produce that we had been paying for and she had been stashing in her digs.

My father apparently gave her a dressing down (we didn't witness this, I heard about it years later) and may have threatened to fire her though she wasn't his servant to dismiss. Having grown up with amahs he knew they were a law unto themselves and not really to be messed with. He figured if he punished her she might take some sort of revenge. What would she do? Poison us? She was in charge of the kitchen so I guess that was possible. She belonged to the flat, this was her world, and we would soon be moving on so he left her alone and kept an eye on the comprador's dockets to make sure her pilfering had ceased.

It was unnerving to have a stranger around like that, a kind of lurking *éminence grise*, albeit one dressed in black and white.

A week or so into our new life I was enrolled at Kowloon Junior School, which was a British international primary school in Perth Street, Ho Man Tin, next to King George V School where I would eventually spend my first two years of high school.

Apparently the school regarded incoming children from Australia as backward. I'm not sure if they used that word but according to my father they thought we had only recently climbed down from the trees and begun walking upright. So it was suggested I have tutoring to prepare me for the obviously superior British system, the coming autumn term and the beginning of Year 3. Tutoring a kid to prepare for Grade 3 sounds extreme but my parents did as they were told and hired a tutor – one suggested by the school, an Indian man who wore flashy clothes and reeked of cheap cologne. I remember him well because he was the most exotic individual I had ever met.

On his first visit he brought with him, rather curiously, a little felt-lined jewellery case full of precious stones. Well, he *claimed* they were precious. They were pretty dazzling and he insisted I hold some of them. A few were sitting on the felt, others wrapped in special soft cloth, and he unveiled them as if revealing the long-lost crown jewels of some mysterious maharaja.

Then my mother came over. "Madam," he said, producing what looked like an emerald. It was green at least. He also had some jade. I guess he was hoping Mum would buy something although that was never articulated and, though polite, she didn't take the bait. This gentleman came twice a week for a little while and over the course of two months I spent many excruciating hours as he tried to unravel the mysteries of mathematics for me, which despite his efforts I have never quite fathomed.

During those lessons I was distracted by sheer boredom and distaste for the subject and by the pet white mouse my father had bought for us not long after we moved in. It lived in a little mouse's house that had a glass front and two levels of tiny space within. Upstairs the mouse slept in a miniature bed of straw. Downstairs was a little wire wheel that he ran on and there he spent his days going nowhere, fast. This was my first experience of the utter futility of existence.

The rodent was called Mousie Tung, my father's little joke poking fun at Mao Tse-tung. During that Cold War era, colonials in Hong Kong liked to ridicule the Chinese leader. It allayed their fear.

I made a few friends at St George's Court. On the first day there my mother had taken me down to the small playground that clung to the hillside beside the apartment buildings. The playground was surrounded by a high wire cage which looked as if it could have been a chimpanzee enclosure at some zoo. A steep stairway led down to a small gravelled platform where there were a set of swings and a slippery dip. I hovered at the top of the stairs with my mother urging me to walk down and join the boys at play who were throwing themselves around like, well, chimps.

They froze and looked up at us as we faltered at the top of the stairs. They exuded a kind of street toughness that made me reluctant to move. It was like a scene from *West Side Story* without the knives.

"Can Phillip come down and play with you boys?" my mother asked rather pathetically. They shrugged and she took that as a yes, albeit a reluctant one.

This gang was made up of kids from the British Isles who lived in the flats above. Gordon and Duncan Wilson were Scots and another boy I got to know later lived here whose mother was Scottish. His name was Mark Coombes and one day he achieved legendary status for making his amah faint. He had bought a trick finger in a shop downtown, a fake-bloodied severed digit made out of rubber that he put on the chopping block in his kitchen. He had taken out the meat cleaver and made a chopping sound followed by a mock scream of pain, placing the fake finger on the block next to it. The amah came running and just fainted dead away, right there on the tiled floor.

I got to know an American kid too. He didn't actually live at St George's Court but next door in a bungalow-style home at the very top of Kadoorie Ave. just before you entered the driveway. His name was Willie Whitlock and his father wore Bermuda shorts, the sort that British men in the colony would never be seen in. I remember Willie playing golf in his front yard wearing swimming togs and gumboots. He had a sister, Denise, whose smile was dazzling because she had a mouth full of steel braces.

My parents also made a few new friends, including an American man who worked for the CBS news network, or so he said. I remember him sitting in the living room of our leave flat one day talking in hushed tones about Vietnam. The conflict there was escalating fast. He had been flying over the country filming from military planes. He spoke in a worrying tone and of course he was right on the money because things were about to get a whole lot worse. Looking back now I don't think he was a CBS cameraman at all. I reckon he was a spy, a CIA spook. It certainly makes a better story.

In our first weeks at St George's Court my dad took me for my first Hong Kong haircut. We went to a Chinese barber down the hill in nearby Mongkok, which is where my father had his office before he upgraded to Tsim Sha Tsui, the pointy bit of Kowloon Peninsula. For many years Mongkok has been the most densely populated place on earth. My father loved its hustle and bustle. We have stayed there in recent years and it's still as vibrant as ever, closer to the old Hong Kong than some of the tourist areas. Many Europeans in the Sixties shunned Mongkok for being "too Chinese". Too Chinese in Hong Kong?

Being an old Hong Kong hand with a pretty respectable grasp of Cantonese, my father embraced Mongkok. I remember arriving at that barber-shop to see one barber placing a bowl on the top of a boy's head. He proceeded to trim the hair sticking out from under the bowl. It was literally a bowl cut. I was horrified and close to gagging from the smell of bay rum, that pungent cologne they used in barber-shops back then.

At six I was already pretty vain and back at the flat I looked at the mirror in horror on seeing that I had been virtually scalped. My mother complained it was a bit severe; my father was unmoved.

It was at St George's Court during that long summer, waiting for the new school term to begin, that I had my pop music awakening. My parents had given me a little transistor radio and I started listening to the pop stations, including BBC radio, piped out from London to Honkers.

Love Me Do, P.S. I Love You and other songs were favourites. It was the beginning of a pop music obsession and the music of the Fab Four would become the soundtrack of my Hong Kong childhood. Our arrival coincided with the rise of the band and our departure in late 1969 – the end of our Hong Kong idyll – marked The Beatles' break-up.

Towards the end of those languid months at St George's Court I was listening to my transistor one day while my mother showed my baby brother Mousie Tung. In bright sunshine Mousie was running for his life on his little wheel.

My brother pawed at the glass, fascinated by the little rodent. And then, somehow, he managed to lift the glass front an inch or two in his effort to get to the sleek little critter inside.

Sensing an opportunity for freedom Mousie Tung jumped off his wheel and darted forward, making a break for it.

He got to the opening and gave the fresh air a tentative sniff, whiskers twitching with excitement. My mother shrieked as Mousie Tung put his head outside and at that precise moment my little brother let the little glass window go.

Unfortunately Mousie was underneath and the falling glass wall acted like a guillotine as it dropped on his neck. My mother screamed, my brother cried, then my sister, who was sitting nearby, also began crying as Ah Chan rushed into the room to witness the gory spectacle.

At my mother's request Ah Chan put the mouse in an old shoebox. The amah wanted to just put it in the bin. Mum refused and said it could lie in its shoebox coffin until my father got home.

When he arrived a few hours later he made some comment about the appropriateness of the execution considering whom the mouse had been named after.

He then took the little white body which he launched into space, flinging it from the balconied heights of Ho Man Tin. It plummeted, spiralling in mid-air, and was soon out of sight.

Mousie Tung was dead whereas Mao Tse-tung was very

much alive and would cast a shadow over our lives in Hong Kong for years to come.

CHAPTER 3

LORD ROBERTS OF THE ORIENT

It wasn't until many years after his death that I found out my English grandfather was a Lord. We knew him simply as Grandad Bob, a somewhat remote figure who popped in and out of our peripatetic lives. I can't remember ever actually speaking to him as we were very small when he was around. I do remember him for one reason – a bizarre party trick. When he had drunk too much, or enough, at family gatherings he used to drop his trousers in front of everyone … revealing the big Bombay bloomers that he used to wear underneath. He would wiggle his hips and drop them down to his knees before pulling them up again. While doing this he would sing an old American folk song, *Hallelujah, I'm a Bum*, a tune in praise of the life of a hobo. God knows where he picked that up: he had wandered far and wide in this world. My father also used to sing that song so the refrain is imprinted on my memory:

Hallelujah, I'm a bum
Hallelujah, bum again
Hallelujah give us a handout
To revive us again.

Not exactly what you'd expect from a Lord, I agree. The thing is that he was really a Lord in name only. His name was Lord Roberts Brown. He was born in Wandsworth, South London, in 1900 and was named after the famous British soldier Lord Roberts, who had distinguished himself in the Boer War and in Afghanistan where he was known as Lord Roberts of Kandahar – and was also known (if not to his face) as Bobs. He was at one stage commander-in-chief of the British Army in the glory days of Empire when Queen Victoria was on the throne and Britannia still ruled the waves.

Whenever I'm in Sydney I think of him because there's a Lord Roberts Hotel in Darlinghurst.

I wonder if my great-grandparents named him Lord Roberts Brown with an eye to a future life somewhere exotic that the Union Jack flew, where having that rather aristocratic moniker on a passport might come in handy? Surely it could only have been to his advantage to have been mistaken for a Lord.

Though he was a touch imperious at times he certainly didn't have the bearing of an aristocrat and his accent wasn't plummy at all. I think in some ways he was pretty true to his working-class South London roots although he did get to live like a Lord out East.

I remember him as a bloke with greyish skin; a somewhat hollow, haunted look, with fingers stained brown from all those cigarettes he smoked.

Not long after we arrived in Hong Kong he turned up too, which made Dad – who spent much of his life trying to emulate and excel his father – uneasy.

My grandfather was the one who had established Hong

Kong as the family seat in the first place so I guess it was natural that he wanted to be back in on the action if the Browns were to have a Hong Kong renaissance. He and my grandmother took a small flat near our leave flat. It's funny the things you remember about people you spent so little time with. I recollect that my grandmother Christina May, or Chris, whom we knew as just Nanny, liked a drink (it's a family trait) and that she knitted incessantly. As the needles flew she would poke out her tongue with her false teeth dangling from the end of it, then suck them back in again without missing a stitch. It was horrifying and fascinating in equal measure and we would sit waiting for it to happen, as it did every few minutes. It was like watching the cuckoo pop out from a cuckoo clock.

So there they were in our St George's Court home, my grandfather puffing away and talking big about the future in Hong Kong; Nanny knitting and flashing her dentures; and Mum looking tense, as she always did when my father's parents were around.

'Demanding' was the word she used to describe them. All those years in the Orient had ruined them for ordinary life, I guess. Dad was uncomfortable, too, because he hadn't really figured his father into the equation. He had thought "the old man", as he called him, might just retire in Sydney and leave Hong Kong to him. One king would abdicate, leaving the throne free for the rightful heir. No way, my grandfather wasn't missing out on another shot at glory in the colony.

That the Browns were back was news and *The South China Morning Post* reported on their return: two civil engineers who had a hand in Hong Kong's reconstruction after World War II had returned to capitalise on the new building boom. Whereas

Hong Kong always seems to be booming, in the 1960s the modern metropolis was emerging, its population swelling as refugees poured across the border escaping Communist China. They lived in ramshackle squatter cities around the perimeter of Kowloon and in the New Territories beyond. The British government in this Eastern outpost was trying to build public housing as fast as it could to accommodate them and my father aimed to cash in on that, though he wanted to be his own man without his old man looking over his shoulder.

But Grandad Bob was colonial royalty and the newspaper story on them both outlined Lord Roberts Brown's long association with Hong Kong. That he'd been a POW there gave him added cachet.

It appears he first arrived there in 1937 although the dates are a bit fuzzy. His journeys into Empire began when he was in his twenties. As a young civil engineer he started out in London before working for the British Steel Piling Co. in Africa and India. Afterwards he kept drifting east and one of my cousins found a record of one of those journeys, on a ship called the *Alsea*. That voyage – from Penang to Siam, now Thailand – sounds like something out of Somerset Maugham. By then he was working for the East Asiatic Co. Ltd.

Eventually he made it as far as Shanghai where he practised his speciality – foundation work – for other foreign companies before starting his own, the China Construction Co. In the Roaring Twenties, Shanghai – known as the Paris of the East – was a bustling, international city with glamorous hotels lining The Bund, a glittering nightlife and a burgeoning film industry.

He had married my grandmother, Christina Cockram, in 1921 and despite his travels they managed to have eight children. It seemed that on each journey home he would impregnate his wife, return to the Orient, and head back to England only to find there was another mouth to feed. Then off he'd go again. My grandmother got a bit sick of being left alone in South London while he was swanning around Shanghai so she insisted on joining him in the Far East with their youngest, Cyril.

Five of the children, including my father, were left at home in London. My grandmother had a baby in Shanghai, Margaret, who died during infancy; and then another, my Aunty Kathleen, who survived.

Uncle Cyril told me once that his mother never quite got over the death of her baby. Despite a lifelong ambition to visit Shanghai and try to find his baby sister's grave, he never did. He said the baby's death changed my grandmother.

"That was the beginning of … you know," and he raised an imaginary glass to his lips, bent his elbow and looked at me knowingly, "but don't you ever put that in print."

The children left behind in London were billeted with an aunt, May. My grandfather, who by now was doing pretty well in Shanghai, constantly wired her money to help her look after them. Sadly, Aunt May was not looking after the children at all. The local authorities reported this to Grandad Bob because it was clear the children were being neglected, living in rags and being fed bread and dripping while May spent the money on herself. So my grandfather bought a house in London for another sister, Maud, and moved the children in with her and her own kids.

Eventually he decided he would make a life for the whole family in the Orient so he brought the five children out to

Shanghai. Eventually, the city became too dangerous as the Japanese were threatening China. Their invasion of Manchuria made my grandfather nervous and with war obviously looming he moved south and set up in Canton where he won a contract to build a waterworks for that southern Chinese city, now known as Guangzhou. As in Shanghai the city had enclaves for Europeans known as foreign concessions. From there the family moved to Portuguese Macau where my grandfather oversaw his next big project … a reservoir. When that was completed he shifted his business to nearby British Hong Kong.

In my study I have a photo of the family from that time in the late Thirties, all dressed in their best Catholic whites. My grandfather was ostensibly Church of England unlike my grandmother, who had Irish heritage as well as English and was quite devout. She had been a novice nun before marrying, and had converted Lord Roberts Brown to Catholicism.

She had a major operation not long after they settled in Hong Kong and my grandfather sent her home to England to recover while he put the children into boarding school. The family home was in mid-Kowloon and the boarding schools were nearby. The boys went to La Salle College, the girls to Maryknoll Convent School.

Uncle Cyril used to tell me stories from their schooldays. My father was scarred by the experience because he was naturally insubordinate and regularly beaten with a strap by the Christian Brothers. Cyril was spared corporal punishment because he was a talented boy soprano, a star of the school choir and a darling of the Brothers.

China Construction Co. soon became a major player in Hong Kong and my grandfather was now wealthy. He seemed to have a very bright future in the colony but his timing was never good and the shadow of war was lengthening. The rampaging Japanese army was wreaking deadly havoc in China while in Hong Kong, that British territory at the extremity of South China won from the mainland in two stages – during the Opium Wars, and at the tail-end of the 19th century – people were whistling in the dark and making merry, trying to ignore their impending doom. The European ladies being ferried to their residences on The Peak by sedan chair may have been riven with anxiety yet their gracious lives went on and the tea dances at The Peninsula continued as they always had.

Meanwhile the news out of China was all bad and while business was booming it was increasingly obvious that the family's future in Hong Kong was in doubt. The British authorities began evacuating citizens to Australia and, while he kept his business afloat in the colony, Grandad Bob decided to move the family to the relative safety of the southern continent. In 1940 they boarded the *SS Nanking*, bound for Sydney. I have a little clipping from *The Sydney Morning Herald* in June that year, written by a social columnist who gloried in the byline Goose Feather, announcing their arrival under the heading LARGEST FAMILY.

Largest family to travel by the ship which reached here the week before last was Mrs C.M. Brown and her five children. Mr Brown is managing director of China Construction Company.

Romance blossomed for the eldest daughter, Miss C.M. Brown, on the trip south. She became engaged to Mr A.L. Dalziel of the Shanghai Municipal Police, who came to Australia to enlist.

Grandad Bob had purchased a big Tudor-style house in

Bannerman Street, Cremorne, on Sydney's Lower North Shore, and eventually came and joined the family there.

My father's two older brothers had been sent home to England where they joined the forces. My Uncle Bob joined the British air force. Uncle Harold enlisted in the British Navy.

Once settled in Sydney, my grandfather began looking at opportunities in Australia. But when he received a telegram telling him he had won a major contract back in Honkers he returned. That's the bit of his story that I really find hard to understand. With the Japanese sweeping through China, with the Pacific War imminent, and life in Hong Kong looking increasingly precarious, he returned on business leaving his wife and five of his children behind.

It was a potentially fatal decision. Because it was while he was there that the Japanese attacked – on December 8, 1941, the day after their assault on Pearl Harbour. Hong Kong was defended by the British Army and civilians drafted into a local supporting militia. They formed what was known as The Gin Drinkers' Line during the Battle of Hong Kong which lasted until Christmas Day.

Grandad Bob was one of those gin drinkers, even though his favourite tipple was always Scotch whisky. The Battle of Hong Kong soon became the Fall of Hong Kong, a kind of ill omen for the Fall of Singapore early the following year.

During the final stages of the conflict, as the Japanese swept south through the New Territories, taking Kowloon and then crossing the harbour, my grandfather and some of the other gin drinkers were making their last stand at a place called Shouson Hill on the coast of Deep Water Bay. Grandad

Bob helped complete the building of the military magazines at Shouson Hill. When it was obvious that defeat was inevitable my grandfather met a Catholic priest who gave him the advice that saved his life. As a militia member Grandad Bob was wearing an army-issue singlet. The priest told him to get rid of it at once because if the Japanese thought he was attached to the military they would either shoot him on the spot or take him prisoner. On December 25, when Hong Kong was surrendered to the Japanese, the military prisoners were all marched to Sham Shui Po POW camp on Kowloon side, a hellhole that, while lesser known than the famous Changi in Singapore, was just as grim.

Luckily – if that's the right word – my grandfather was sent to the civilian POW camp at Stanley. The waterfront there is now peppered with pubs and restaurants and I have lunched on that promenade looking out at Stanley Peninsula as I try to imagine what life then must have been like. The book *Prisoners of the East* by Allana Corbin tells stories of life in the Stanley Civilian Internment Camp and of the families interned there. It might have been our whole family if my grandfather hadn't moved them to Australia in time.

All this while his wife and children fretted in their big Sydney house with no money and a breadwinner who was now a prisoner of the Japanese. Although they didn't know he was; they thought he was dead. Because when the list of Europeans who had died in the Fall of Hong Kong was published, my grandfather's name was on it. Turns out there was another L.R. Brown who had died defending the colony.

Everyone thought it was Grandad Bob. Apparently when my grandmother read that she swooned and took to her bed, weeping piteously for weeks and singing *Ave Maria* in her sleep, presumably to comfort herself.

Then, a few months later she got a telegram from the Red Cross announcing that my grandfather hadn't died after all and was, instead, a POW at Stanley.

This must have been some relief to the family although there was a problem. Somehow they had to survive the war years with no visible means of support. At that stage my father was a pupil at Mosman Public School although things came to a head there after he was caned one day. Dad, who was a bit of a tough guy, spent much of his time at school brawling with other students who picked on him because he was a Pom from Hong Kong. Following that final caning he had taken the cane out of his headmaster's hands and broken it in two. That didn't go down well. He was promptly expelled which he always said didn't worry him in the slightest. He then went to work to support his mother, getting a job in a fridge factory owned by the well-known Sydney businessman Sir Edward Holstrom, who had a hand in establishing Taronga Park Zoo.

Then, in January 1943, he joined the Australian Army after Sir Edward signed papers testifying he was eighteen. He was actually seventeen.

He joined the 2/14 Battalion, which had distinguished itself in Syria and on the Kokoda Track. He was sent to the jungle warfare training centre at Canungra in the hinterland behind what is now the Gold Coast. Later he was based in North Queensland. Dad almost missed out on active duty, eventually seeing action in one of the last battles of the Pacific War. As part of Operation Oboe, his battalion was shipped from Townsville to Borneo where they executed a major beach landing as part of the Battle of Balikpapan which raged for three weeks in July 1945.

A constant reminder of that battle is the samurai sword my father liberated from a deceased Japanese NCO. It is still in immaculate condition. I sometimes ask myself should I try to find the family it belonged to but am not sure I could ever part with it. It's an amazing artefact that reminds me of my dad and makes me wonder what he went through in that battle. He may have been a Pom from Hong Kong but serving in the Australian Army changed all that, I think. I'm certain that's what turned him into an Aussie.

Grandad Bob still languished in the POW camp at Stanley as my father and his comrades hit the beach in Borneo. The Peninsula became the headquarters of Japan's occupying force in Hong Kong right through until it surrendered at Government House in 1945.

And here's where serendipity really comes into play. Following the surrender a British ship, the first into Hong Kong after the war, came to pick up POWs. It was the *HMS Maidstone*, a submarine resupply vessel. One of the crew happened to be my Uncle Harold, who was an ordinary seaman.

The Hong Kong newspapers found out about this and ran a story about how Harold went to Stanley and emerged from the camp there carrying his emaciated, half dead father, by piggyback.

Then the *Maidstone*, with its POW 'cargo', sailed down past The Philippines, stopping at Makassar to pick up more. She sailed further south to Fremantle where they were given a tremendous welcome, then on to Sydney where my grandmother was waiting dockside at Circular Quay.

Uncle Cyril, who was a teenager at the time, remembers the anticipation as they craned their necks, scouring the faces as the surviving POWs straggled onto the dock. Nanny couldn't spot my grandfather. After a time someone tapped her on the shoulder and she turned to find a walking skeleton she barely recognised. "It's me, Bob," he said and she burst into tears, throwing her arms around him as my uncle looked on, tears streaming down his face too.

Once he had recovered, the family returned home to England, settling for a time at Bognor Regis while Grandad Bob negotiated war reparations with the British government. He had been working for them when Hong Kong fell and lost everything, including all his machinery, and wanted compensation so he could start up again. The family could have stayed in England had they not been away too long and no longer felt English after so many years spent in the Far East and Australia.

So when he got his money the family moved back to Hong Kong. He went to see Sir Arthur Morse, head of the Hong Kong and Shanghai Banking Corporation, got himself a hefty overdraft and started over. They lived first at Repulse Bay on Hong Kong side. Then the family took up residence at 5 Dorset Crescent in the gracious garden suburb of Kowloon Tong, an enclave of stately homes at the foot of Lion Rock. The house was opposite the one in Devon Road where we spent the best of our years in Hong Kong in the 1960s. Life was good and just got better and better. China Construction Co. got major contracts, including one to build a Shell Oil installation on the Kowloon Bay shore. My grandfather bought a converted minesweeper and christened it *The Elephant*, which I think had something to do with those pink elephants you supposedly see when you are drunk. The family sailed around the harbour throwing gin parties on board and I have some grainy family film footage of one of them. It looks like something out of an old Noël Coward movie.

My father always talked fondly of those years. They lived the high life. Dad fancied himself something of a playboy and there is a box of family photos showing him with different young women at dazzling Hong Kong parties. I have a Peninsula Hotel dinner menu from that time … the Hong Kong Football Club's annual dinner dance. The entrée was clear turtle soup, the main course fried garoupa (a local delicacy) followed by roast beef with Charlotte russe cake to follow.

In those post-war years Dad played rugby for the Hong Kong Football Club and represented the colony in the Interport Rugby series. His rugby album still sits on a shelf near my desk and sometimes I open it to look at the amazing photos of those colonial glory days and the players with their beards and baggy shorts. One of the highlights, my father once recalled, was a game against the French, played in Shanghai in the snow.

But, well as things were going, Grandad Bob was worried about the Communists who were fighting to gain control of China from Generalissimo Chiang Kai-shek's Nationalist army. He had employed a lot of former Nationalist troops who had fled to Hong Kong and what he heard from them unsettled him.

When the Communists finally won and declared the People's Republic in 1949 Grandad Bob was worried, very worried. He told his sons that, bad as the Japanese were, the Communists were more to be feared. He warned them: "If they ever capture me I will kill myself."

What if they did take Hong Kong? It wasn't impossible. Hong Kong was British but it was largely a trophy of the Opium Wars and the Chinese had always resented that. And The New Territories was only leased from China anyway. My grandfather didn't trust the Chinese to honour the lease and Hong Kong had been part of China before so why wouldn't they just take it back?

Fearful of that, he panicked and made the momentous decision to quit Hong Kong and come to Australia, which had sheltered his family during the war.

And so the family immigrated to Sydney in 1951. And that changed everything. We would now be Australian.

That might have been the end of the family's time in Hong Kong were it not for one key thing: my father missed the exotic life there and always yearned to go back. He didn't expect my grandfather to follow him but Hong Kong has a siren lure.

So there was Grandad Bob in 1963, sitting on our couch in Hong Kong, puffing away and knocking back the Johnnie Walker, settling in for another long stint ... or so he thought. In reality it was too late for him. By then the cancer that would kill him the following year had a grip. He went back to Sydney to die, leaving my father alone in Hong Kong to carry on. Lord Roberts Brown was dead; the Brown dynasty survived.

CHAPTER 4

A GREEN AND PLEASANT LAND

I made an expansive gesture as we sat looking over the verdant grounds of the Kowloon Cricket Club, a motion of the type often followed by something like … "My son, one day all this will be yours."

Sandra's eyes glazed over as I nodded approvingly at the vision splendid and looked around at Hamish for confirmation.

"And?" she said.

It wasn't really a question; it was more of a statement. What she meant was …"So what?"

To me this verdant patch, this little corner of a foreign land that is forever colonial Hong Kong, is heaven. In the middle of Kowloon occupying real estate that would be worth a motza, the Kowloon Cricket Club – or the KCC as everyone knows it – is one of my touchstones.

Visiting the KCC is a ritual I enact every time I visit Hong Kong, which is every two or three years, just to keep the fantasy going.

Such stops are like Stations of the Cross for me. The solemn ceremonial procession through them always starts with

The Peninsula, of course. That hotel is the cathedral of my childhood and I worship there with the ardent devotion of any true believer. I would burn joss sticks in the foyer if I could.

The stations on my pilgrimage route are remnants of my boyhood and all the more precious considering how much has been swept away as progress has reshaped the place. They are relics of bygone days that persist even as Hong Kong changes, almost before our eyes. Skyscrapers soar; incessant reclamation expands Kowloon; superhighways and tunnels are built in the time it would take elsewhere to decide on building them. Despite all that, some things remain and I'm thankful it is so. Accordingly I return to these stubborn symbols of old Hong Kong in the same way Buddhists might visit a temple that claims to have a tooth or a bone from Siddhartha Gautama's big toe under some stupa.

After The Peninsula is ticked off, my second place of worship is usually Swindon Book Co. a couple of streets away in Lock Road, Tsim Sha Tsui, a shortish thoroughfare of cafés and teahouses that runs between Haiphong and Peking Streets.

It comforts me no end that it is still there, just across the road from the Marks & Spencer food hall where we stock up with treats for our hotel room to circumvent room service prices and the outrageous costs of the mini-bar. When I wander down Lock Rd and see Swindon where it has always been I feel that all is right with the world.

As a boy I spent countless hours in that bookshop. Now when I visit I usually wander back in with – to quote the poet Philip Larkin – a kind of '*awkward reverence*', like an old monk returning to the monastery where he started out as a novice all those years ago. I will usually walk in and inhale a whiff of the rarefied air, hoping it will trigger memory. On one visit I did that a little too obviously and the proprietor looked up to see me sniffing, my nose in the air, as if there was some suspect pong wafting through his shop.

"Why are you sniffing?" my wife had asked.

"To smell the books," I said. "And the smell is still here." Or am I just imagining things?

I do believe that bookshop has a unique signature fragrance because fresh books have their own distinct aroma. I remember exactly how those little hardback Hardy Boys crime novels I used to buy smelt. And if I close my eyes I can still catch the scent of those C.S. Lewis ones too and the H. Rider Haggard African adventure stories I loved … *King Solomon's Mines, She, Allan Quatermain* and the others, all terrific stories that would be deemed politically incorrect now.

I bought my first little volume of Kafka's short stories at Swindon when I was twelve and had nightmares about waking up and finding I had turned into a cockroach. So each time I visit Hong Kong I always come away with a little trophy, a new Swindon memento, mostly something from its table of books about Hong Kong – illustrated histories, compendiums of travellers' tales and denser political histories that I set aside to read later yet never quite get to.

As that familiar fragrance fills my nostrils I browse until moved along by my wife and son whose patience has its limits, unlike my penchant for self-indulgence in the search for lost time in my old hometown.

On my most recent visit I thought I might impress the bloke behind the counter by telling him about my Swindon pedigree, how I had been coming there since the mid-Sixties.

If I wasn't expecting a plaque or a small bronze statue of myself to be erected in the window or anything, nor was I completely prepared for the kind of diffidence I was met with. I obviously hadn't read him very well. Ignoring my effusions about the history of the shop that was now the venue for his day job, my man didn't even look up as he calculated my bill and when he'd done that all he said was: "You pay Hong Kong dollar or Australian?"

"Hong Kong dollars is fine," I said, handing him my credit card.

A visit back to Kowloon Tong, our final place of residence in Hong Kong, is usually on the agenda. On the pavement outside our old home at 7 Devon Rd I will stand and peer through the gates like some burglar casing the joint.

Kowloon Cricket Club is another must and, for me, a palpable, living museum. In Hong Kong everyone has to have a club. Ours was always the Kowloon Cricket Club and the family connection dates back to the 1930s when my grandfather first joined. The club, established in 1904, is one of those rare historical remnants that have escaped the wrecking ball. Rapacious development has destroyed many an old landmark: nevertheless, some stubbornly cling on.

In the late Thirties the Browns lived relatively close to the club on Prince Edward Road and the club, along with The Peninsula, was integral to their social whirl. When my grandfather was banged up in Stanley Internment Camp in late 1941 the club suffered too. While most of its members had fled or were imprisoned it was deserted, and looters who soon stripped everything of value from it even took the doors and window frames. The wooden flooring was ripped up and converted into firewood. The clubhouse and main cricket ground were used by the Japanese invaders for stabling their horses and mules during those bleak war years.

The ground was eventually rejuvenated in the years after World War II (although apparently it took a few years for the cricket pitch to fully recover) and the family, then living in Kowloon Tong, continued their long association with the place, picking up where they'd left off as everyone who survived the war tended to do.

One of the first things Dad did after our arrival in Hong Kong in 1963 was to renew his membership of the KCC. And soon we began our ritual attendances there. That first summer was long, hot and tedious due to water shortages so the KCC swimming pool was a place to escape, and our Sixties summers – or the portion of them when we weren't back in Australia or travelling around Asia – were spent poolside there. Ask anyone who frequented the KCC pool fifty years ago what their favourite memory is and I'll bet at least half of them will mention, like me, the samosas they used to serve at the little cabana there. Those little spicy, ever so slightly greasy, triangles are legendary and were perfect washed down with a Coke or a Pepsi, or a bottle of Green Spot, an orange-flavoured drink that was one of us kids' favourite tipples.

When I visit the KCC now I watch families wending their way along the path that runs from the clubhouse and along the edge of the tree-shaded cricket ground, and I can see us doing the very same thing five long decades ago.

If you're looking for it you'll find it in Cox's Road, Jordan, near the old Gun Club Hill Barracks where the British Army was located. We used to play soccer against the army kids who went to school there and they were among our toughest opponents. Next to Gun Club Hill is the United Services Recreation Club, the USRC, another club popular among the European set. These clubs had relatively few Chinese members in the colonial era (the USRC had none at all). That has completely changed now, as it should have. I went to birthday parties at the USRC as a kid, though we were never members there.

The KCC remains an enclave that still evokes Empire despite its modern touches. It's a green oasis in Kowloon – sacred ground to me – and it must be charmed to have resisted the development of modern Hong Kong. Nowadays the club has international cachet as the home of the Hong Kong Cricket Sixes competition held in late October and early November. I've never been in Hong Kong when it's on but hope to time a future visit to coincide with it.

Sandra and Hamish are never as keen as I about making the pilgrimage to the KCC on our Hong Kong visits. Nonetheless they go along, if a tad reluctantly, and I like to think deep down they do enjoy their time there.

Besides, the KCC is not a stuffy club, not a place full of cigar-puffing ancient Hong Kong hands reminiscing about the olden days when the Union Jack still fluttered in the monsoonal breezes.

One of the biggest get-togethers back in the Sixties was its annual New Year's Day bash which included a sports programme for families. We all competed in a raft of events – sack races, three-legged races, egg-and-spoon races; and there was always a tug-of-war. Not the sort of events you'd hold in midsummer but around New Year it was always cool. Some people think Hong Kong is humid and tropical all year round: in fact it gets surprisingly chilly in winter. We used to rug up for the New Year's Day fun, my father cheering us on from the sidelines in corduroy trousers, wearing one of his tailored shirts and a cashmere cardigan, with his customary cravat. The cardigans got bigger each year as his girth expanded, reflecting his success, as Chinese custom would have it. Some called him '*Fei Jai*' ('Fat Boy') in a joking, endearing way because as he got rounder, and his hairline receded further, he grew to resemble one of those chubby laughing Buddhas, the ones whose tummies you rub for good luck.

Somewhere I have a photo of me, my Aussie mate Tim Budge and my pal Greg England all straining away at a length of thick rope on one of those New Year's Days. After the kids' activities, the early evening featured a smorgasbord and a raffle. One year my father won virtually all the prizes and people groaned as each one was announced with the winner being, yet again, Ted Brown. We were all amazed at his luck. It turned out he had bought most of the tickets.

One year the English cricket team put on a display match there and I got their autographs on a signed programme that I kept in a bottom drawer for years. Do you think I can find it now?

When Uncle Cyril was back in Hong Kong in the Eighties working as a supervising engineer on the brand new MTR (Mass Transit Railway) we dined at the KCC every second night, feasting on one of the signature dishes, Singapore noodles, which is still on the menu. Their Singapore noodles are excellent.

Nowadays I email the club before each arrival, explaining

the family connection and making sure we're expected because I wouldn't want the shame of being turned away because I'm not a current member. I'm always told we will be welcome to come in, have coffee or lunch and look around. Part of the ritual is that each time we go to the KCC I buy a souvenir, often one of their polo shirts with the distinctive club crest on it ... the nine squiggly little green dragons that symbolise Kowloon.

On one trip to Hong Kong in the early 1990s we met Alec Reeve – the father of my childhood pal Mark – for lunch at the KCC. I had rung him out of the blue and he had kindly come in from his home at Discovery Bay on Lantau Island to meet Sandra and me for lunch. Mr Reeve was assistant headmaster during my two years at King George V School which was a bit embarrassing because I was close mates with Mark and often at their King's Park flat after school. I felt a little intimidated by having the assistant headmaster look me over, particularly since I managed to get myself in so much trouble in those two years. On one visit to his home Mr Reeve pulled me aside and said, basically, what happens at school stays at school and I wasn't to be concerned because I was always welcome. I have always remembered that act of kindness.

Mr Reeve replaced Mr Gore as headmaster and went on to become well known and much loved as an educator of so many expat kids. Every year at the KCC they play for the Alec Reeve Memorial Trophy.

When we lunched with him at the KCC I found myself wondering halfway through if he really did remember me from all those years ago or was just being polite. At times he seemed a bit vague and frustrated as he clutched at memories. A year or two afterwards I found out that he had developed Alzheimer's and that our KCC lunch must have been on the cusp of his illness, before he entered that final twilight zone. He died in Hong Kong a few years after our meeting and I'm grateful we had that opportunity to lunch with him before he went gentle into that good night.

And I'm equally grateful the KCC is still there to rekindle such memories, an *aide-mémoire* reminding old colonials of a lost world.

Your welcome at the KCC is always a warm one.

Although there was one incident some years ago. …

On this occasion we had walked from Yau Ma Tei in the heat. I was flustered because we had visited the Tin Hau Temple there, a Taoist complex near the famous jade market. The complex includes a shrine to Kwun Yam, or Kuan Yin as she is also known – the Goddess of Mercy.

While we were there a fortune-teller told me that I was angry, which made me, er, cross. Having arrived hot and flustered at the KCC, now we were pleased to find that, yes, the manager was expecting us and, yes, we could come in. So we sat down at a veranda table overlooking the cricket field and ordered some coffee. We had an hour before a lunch engagement next door at the USRC to which some Hong Kong friends had invited us for a poolside lunch.

I'd had my obligatory browse in the shop on the way in and purchased yet another KCC polo shirt along with vouchers for our coffee, which we sipped as we sat overlooking the striking expanse of green. I was sitting there soaking up the ambience and the air conditioning – quite possibly banging on about the good old days – when I felt a slight tingling in my pocket, the momentary warning of an incoming call on my mobile. No big deal, right? Wrong.

Clubs in Hong Kong are notorious for their rules. Go to the KCC website and you'll find, under the Club By-Laws section – a modern version of Hammurabi's Laws – one stipulating there is to be no use of electronic devices in the clubhouse. Especially phones. Breaking these by-laws is sinful in the extreme as I was soon to find out.

As the phone rang I grappled for it and as I did so heads began turning. Faces that were laughing only moments earlier were now solemn masks, frowning in my direction. I looked up to see the café manager make a beeline for our table. He had a face like thunder and started wagging his finger at me on his way over. As he got closer he half shouted, "No phone! No phone!"

Wearing baggy shorts, I was still digging the pulsating device out of my pocket when he finally reached the table. He was as furious as a man would be if you had just insulted his wife, mother and entire family tree.

"No phone!" he said again, only louder this time. "Owside, please, owside!"

I quickly turned it to silent. Still it kept vibrating so I promptly got up and went out into the foyer. Not in the least placated, he followed me out and as I put it to my ear he pointed and shouted again. "Owside!" he said, indicating that I was to take the call outside the clubhouse entirely. Although I've since learnt that there are some booths just off the foyer for nefarious phone calling but I wasn't aware of that at the time.

It was a friend from Brisbane calling, a friend who hadn't realised I was overseas.

"What are you doing in Hong Kong?" he said.

"Well, at the moment I'm getting thrown out of my own club," I answered.

Sandra and Hamish came outside and joined me in the driveway.

"Well, that was quite a scene," Sandra said.

"Yes," I replied. "Sorry. I forgot about the phone rule."

For a moment I considered trying to go back in after hanging up, then I looked at my watch. It was nearly time for lunch, so better to cut and run. We walked along Jordan Road to the USRC and met up with my friend Liam Fitzpatrick and his family. Liam works for *Time* magazine in Hong Kong and had invited us to his club for a bite and a swim.

I told him about the ugly scene at the KCC and he assured me the USRC was more relaxed.

"Hopefully I can keep out of trouble here," I said.

I then had to get changed into my swimming trunks (Sandra and Hamish were already wearing their costumes underneath their clothes) so I wandered off to the change rooms behind the pool.

As I wended my way past the pool, padding around the fringe of green mesh that formed its perimeter, I saw the lifeguard coming towards me with an angry look on his face. I had seen that look before.

"Keep away," he said, using the sort of literal English Cantonese people sometimes employ. "No walking on poolside. You must go around."

There was no please or thank you attached to that, by the way.

Quickly I changed tack, giving the pool a wider berth. I went and got changed.

When I got back to the table I sat down with a touch of resignation.

"You just can't win," my wife said.

"Rules are rules," I intoned. I went over and dived into the pool although I'm not sure if diving is allowed. Oh well. …

CHAPTER 5

AH MOY

The face may be familiar to me. Still it's the face of a stranger. Each time I flick through my photo album there she is, our amah, Ah Moy. It means 'Little Sister'. I have only one photo of her and I guess I'm lucky to have that. Not everyone took photos of their servants in that epoch. My father was a shutterbug, though, so I do have something of a photographic treasure trove of my Hong Kong childhood. I often sift through them and wonder, *Were we really there?* It was long ago and far away and sometimes seems like it happened to someone else altogether.

In the photo that features Ah Moy she is not the subject, of course, and part of her is out of the frame which seems symbolic. Even so, it's the only record I have of her. The photo was taken in the driveway of our second house in Hong Kong, in La Salle Road, Kowloon. My sister and I are front and centre, the two Chinese people in it being rather incidental. I stand holding hands with my sister, Jane. In the background is our driver, whose name I cannot remember. He was our first driver in Hong Kong. We never called them chauffeurs: I imagine a chauffeur would probably wear a uniform and a hat. This fellow, middle-aged with a salt-and-pepper crew cut, is shown opening the car door preparatory to heading off on a jaunt somewhere. His trousers are pulled up above his waist and he has his tie tucked into a white shirt. He's looking at my father take the photo as the realisation dawns that he is going to be in it.

My sister and I are posing and she is smiling. I am not quite smiling, which is fairly typical. I spent my childhood being told to smile for photos by my father but have always had a disinclination to convey confected happiness and that kicked in early. So usually I am pouting. In this photo my face expresses a vague disconcertion.

Next to us, standing to attention, is Ah Moy, our live-in amah for several years, who was there day and night for most of that time. A woman we never really knew.

After the rigours of Ah Chan at the leave flat in St George's Court we moved to La Salle Rd, not far from the school my father and his brothers attended on the eve of World War II when the family first came to Kowloon. Only recently I found out that later Bruce Lee went to that same school, which to my mind adds a certain prestige.

When I was living in Melbourne in the early 1990s I wrote something for *The Australian* about Hong Kong and mentioned my family background. After it was published I received a call from a Portuguese man who lived in Melbourne.

"I knew some Browns at La Salle College in the late 1930s," he said. "Are you related to Cyril Brown by any chance?" That was a bolt from the blue. He had been in my uncle's year and shared a dormitory with him. Those colonial connections pop up every now and then.

I guess it was probably late 1963 when we moved to La Salle Rd, shortly after I had started at Kowloon Junior School. We weren't there that long so it registers as more of a fleeting memory. The leave flat was a bit grander but it was someone else's house and we didn't really feel we belonged there. And I'm sure the glowering Ah Chan was glad to see the back of us.

Obviously we needed an amah – all Westerners had amahs back then – and this was when Ah Moy came into our lives. Most amahs were single women, many of whom had come from China, escaping poverty and the upheavals that led up to the Cultural Revolution. In the rural areas of Guangdong province just across the border, these women originally worked in the silk trade. When the silk boom ended they formed sisterhoods and dedicated themselves to domestic service.

They were like nuns who gave their lives over to a vocation and they even wore their own nun's habits – the traditional black-and-white uniforms that marked them as servants. Since the late 1940s they had left rural China for Hong Kong where they worked as live-in housemaids, sending money home to their families. They were independent, eschewed marriage and worshipped the chaste goddesses Tin Hau and Kuan Yin.

The etymology of the word 'amah' may have originated from the Portuguese *ama*, meaning 'nurse', though some say it's from the Chinese *ah ma* which means 'little mother' or 'grandmother'.

I'm looking at the photo with Ah Moy in it now. She looks to be in her thirties, although it's hard to tell. She has a thick head of tightly curled black hair forming a kind of helmet. She is brown-skinned, suggestive of her peasant background.

There was something different about Ah Moy that marked

her out as an individual. Unlike Ah Chan and most other amahs – sometimes known as black- and-whites – she eschewed the uniform in favour of a colourful outfit. Her choice was still pyjama-like with that cheongsam-style neck. In the photo I have she is wearing pink slacks and matching top. The outfit has some kind of floral motif blossoming on it. My mother once told me that Dad initially asked Ah Moy to wear the black-and-white and she refused. In theory a servant who refuses a master's request shouldn't last long: for some reason my father acquiesced. Ah Moy was, it seems, a little feisty. She had whatever the Cantonese version of chutzpah was. My parents must have liked that or at least respected it.

What's strange to me is that I recall her presence so clearly and yet I knew – and know – nothing about her. I'm not even sure if my parents knew anything about her and her English was, I recall, quite rudimentary. So here was this woman from another world, another culture, living in our house like a second mother, who was and remains a complete mystery.

We were at fairly close quarters in that house too. It wasn't as spacious as the leave flat and was only a stopgap before we upgraded to Yau Yat Chuen and later Kowloon Tong. La Salle Rd was where we lived, briefly, from late 1963.

It was where we lived as I settled into life at Kowloon Junior School. When I arrived at the school I was briefly a curiosity, because there weren't many Australians there at that time. Most of the children were from the British Isles. Their parents worked for government, the dockyards or the police. British Army kids had their own school so we didn't get to mix with them.

There were also white South Africans and other Caucasians,

including a smattering of Portuguese kids. Macau, just across the water from Hong Kong, had been a Portuguese enclave since the 16th century and many Portuguese from Macau had settled in the British colony. Their names seemed mildly exotic … Ozorio, Jesu, Remedios, d'Almeida. The Portuguese kid I remember best from those early days at Kowloon Junior School was one Dominic d'Amata. The Portuguese all seemed tougher than the other kids – streetwise, with a twang to their accents, and Dominic was nothing short of a punk.

A small boy, he seemed to take a shine to me, if you could call it a shine. Really, I guess he picked on me, and insisted on showing me his judo moves by throwing me onto the ground at various times. The ground in our small playground was bitumen so that hurt.

He also took great delight in showing me how a Chinese burn worked, pinching my skin until I cried out that I'd had enough whereupon he would let go while laughing. "It's enough already," he would say with that Portuguese twang that always sounded a tad American.

There were few Chinese children at the school. In fact I don't remember any when I first arrived although later there was a girl called Elizabeth See in my class. See See, we called her. She was tougher than any of us. And in Grade 5 we had a Chinese teacher, Miss Fung, who was about the size of that pocket rocket singer Lulu, who was popular at the time. Miss Fung was immaculate. She wore amazing tailored suits and hair sculpted into a busby-like beehive do. That hair never moved. Miss Fung insisted on calling me Charlie Brown after the *Peanuts* cartoon strip character and seemed to like me but caused a major embarrassment one day when she accused me of picking my nose in class. I contend that it was a scratch, not a pick, but the damage was done. That was the first time I ever blushed. My friend David McKirdy recalls her as a "Dragon Lady from a James Bond book".

Apart from Elizabeth See and Miss Fung there was nothing much Chinese about the school at all. It was a colonial enclave, like all the other colonial enclaves that existed within the Chinese world of Hong Kong. Even though we orbited that world, ours and theirs hardly ever collided. A high mesh fence separated us from the Chinese school beyond. That other world seemed distant and foreign though the reality of course was that we, not they, were the foreigners.

There were quite a few Americans at the school so, as well as celebrating English customs such as Guy Fawkes Day, there was an annual Halloween event for which we donned fancy dress.

There's a photo of me standing out front of the school in the Hercules outfit my mother had made for Halloween when I was in Grade 4. It was ambitious really, considering my whippet-like physique. Was I aware how ridiculous I looked? I daresay I was.

I'd settled into Grade 3 with relative ease and that was pleasant enough when I wasn't getting roughed up in the playground. In class I spent my time mooning over my art teacher, Miss Bloor. She was English, a bit of a hippy (she may have been a Druid, actually) and I spent an awful lot of my time looking down the front of her dress. She didn't wear a bra, which was kind of fascinating. She looked as though she should've been on the cover of a pop album or in a folk ensemble. She had hair the colour of straw and I may have been in love with her.

She was beguiling in her way but she and all the other teachers were eclipsed by the chief enchantress – our glamorous headmistress, Mrs Versloot. Rosalind Versloot – who married a Dutchman – was a Hong Kong legend and there's a worldwide diaspora of former KJS students who smile, nod and raise their eyebrows knowingly when her name is mentioned. She was unforgettable.

I'm trying to picture her now ... I can see her jet black hair, reminiscent of Elizabeth Taylor as the Egyptian queen in the sprawling sword-and-sandal epic *Cleopatra*.

Mrs Versloot was always heavily made up with blue to purple eyeshadow and bright lipstick, and she wore the most amazing outfits with fishnet stockings. And a mini-skirt: who could forget that? No one could have dressed less like a schoolmarm than Mrs Versloot. Some of her wardrobe was probably by Mary Quant or some other new designer from London. Hong Kong in the Sixties was never far behind in the fashion stakes and Mrs Versloot was the epitome of that. They called the colony Carnaby Street East and she was its poster girl.

Mrs Versloot became headmistress just after I arrived at the school. Some of the mothers raised their eyebrows at her daily fashion statement while the fathers seemed to approve. And we all loved it. It felt like a movie star was running our school.

Flashy as she was, she was daunting too and I admit we were all a little afraid of her. Which may have been how she wanted it.

Her office was just inside the main entrance. The school consisted of two blocks running off to the south and west with the lower grades in the south block and Year 6 upstairs from the head's office. At recess and lunchtime we played in a quadrangle between the blocks and though there was no sports oval we did have access to the facilities at King George V School next door for our sports days and football matches.

Beyond that high mesh fence around our playground the landscape fell away into the Chinese netherworld. Mrs Versloot ruled this little imperial United Nations with an iron hand in a velvet glove, the scent of her perfume trailing behind her.

We were in awe of her and, as I said, a bit scared. That added to the frisson. As boys we may also have been a little besotted. She was aloof though and the only way you would get close to her might be if you were in trouble. Or if, like me one day, you were involved in a medical emergency.

It happened like this. We were skylarking, as boys do (or should) in the playground. I can recall the scene perfectly and locate it in my memory bank by way of a song. Someone with a transistor at school had it on during the break and the song *Glad All Over* by the British pop band The Dave Clark Five was playing with its distinctive drumbeat. It was a huge hit that knocked The Beatles' *I Want to Hold Your Hand* off the top of the charts. Proust had his madeleine cake to twig his recollections; I have songs and books. If I should hear *P.S. I Love You*, for example, I am immediately transported back to our leave flat at St George's Court, sitting in the lounge room playing with a little cloth-sailed wooden junk. The Rolling Stones song *As Tears Go By* is associated with our third home, in Yau Yat Chuen, and The Kinks' *Waterloo Sunset* recalls for me the first moment I heard its nasal drone emanating from our old radiogram as I descended the long stone stairway of our house in Kowloon Tong.

Glad All Over will always take me back to the KJS playground, and the song's title is somewhat ironic considering what it signifies.

Being boys of a certain age, full of beans, we were running amok on this particular day, rushing in and out of the boys' toilets slamming doors and behaving badly, laughing madly and shouting at each other.

A teacher having noticed this was steaming across the bitumen towards us to shut down this behaviour. I ran inside to warn a schoolmate and put my hand in the space next to the hinge of a door when someone promptly came out of that cubicle and slammed the door behind him. On my hand. Or, to be exact, my fingers.

I let out a bloodcurdling scream that echoed in the dank interior and I imagine would have been heard all over the school. The pain was blinding and the boy who had slammed the door looked shocked and immediately ran off.

I emerged holding my hand aloft and a teacher – I'm not sure which one –,looked at it unable to keep a poker face and quickly steered me away from the playground towards the school entrance. I wasn't sure where we were going at first: soon I realised we were heading for the holy of holies, the forbidden land of Mrs Versloot's office. I was ushered inside.

My hand was throbbing, my fingers starting to show signs of severe bruising, and it was obvious that a couple of my fingernails were beginning to lift off. I don't think I was crying: I was in too much shock – shock now tinged with a vague sense of wonderment.

In my juvenile fancy I saw myself as Marc Antony entering Cleopatra's chamber. And Cleopatra was attending to me herself. Mrs Versloot's pervasive scent was unmistakable, even to my untrained nostrils, as she hovered over me like a cross between an angel and a courtesan. I was entranced.

She sat me down and offered words of comfort as she rang for help – not from an ambulance but from my mother, who I could hear on the other end of the line having mild hysterics. We lived nearby so it didn't take her long to arrive in the car with that long-forgotten driver at the wheel.

Waiting for Mum I took in my surroundings. I thought I might be ushered outside to sit in the hall or in some sickroom. Some hope. The headmistress insisted I stay put. She gave me a wet washer to wrap around my hand. I felt like the proverbial spy in the house of love and, despite my throbbing fingers, was almost sad to leave when my mother rushed into the room and then shepherded me out, farewelled by Mrs Versloot who looked terrific as I waved goodbye. The driver was waiting outside with the engine still running. I was bundled into the back seat and then rushed … no, not to a hospital – direct to the good old Pen.

It says a lot about our life then that rather than an emergency ward I was despatched to a luxury hotel. There was a hospital not far from the school, actually – St Theresa's, where my grandfather had been admitted with his cancer before he'd gone home to Australia to die.

We went in the opposite direction, down Nathan Road to the pointy end of Kowloon, where The Peninsula dominated the waterfront in the days before reclamation robbed it of its harbour frontage.

We swung into Salisbury Rd and into the driveway, which is still guarded by those formidable stone lions. Why were we rushing to The Pen in a medical emergency? Simple really. Our doctor's rooms were there. The Peninsula was a bit of a one-stop shop in those days. Our doctor's rooms – and our dentist's – were both located on the first floor. My father's lawyer was up there too and in the arcade running off the foyer was our barber.

As I recollect it our doctor, Dr Wylie, was Scottish. Having obviously been expecting us, he examined my mangled fingers as if he had never seen such a mess and had me dip them into a jar of some yellowish liquid that stung like hell. It was some sort of disinfectant, I guess. This was probably just as well since the injury had occurred in a toilet.

He suggested I would lose a couple of fingernails, hastening to assure me they would grow back soon enough. My fingers were wrapped in gauze, then apparently there wasn't much else to be done. Time would do its healing work, Dr Wylie said.

We went downstairs, then into the foyer, and early lunch was now being served so the place was busy. While Mum grabbed a table I went to the loo, tried to pretend there wasn't a man who looked like a waiter sitting on a chair near the urinals – the aforementioned attendant – and then went back out to the foyer to find Mum.

She was talking to my father who was having some sort of meeting at a table nearby.

My father was relatively dismissive of my injury. My mother and I sat at a table where she had a cup of coffee while I was treated to a Coke float, my favourite tipple at The Pen – a scoop of ice cream in a glass of Coke which would froth up the moment the ice cream was dropped in.

Soothed by the plush surrounds of The Pen's foyer, I felt

the trauma subsiding – a trauma not without a touch of magic simply because it had taken me to Mrs Versloot's office for just a little while. I felt like some traveller in antiquity who had been given an audience with the Queen of Sheba.

Occasionally her name pops up on some of the Hong Kong Facebook groups I'm a member of, and mention of her always elicits much excitement and a flurry of posts.

I have no photos of her though. Just the memory.

I do have a photo of Ah Moy who I can recall fussing over me when we got back from The Pen that day. Her maternal instincts kicked in and she seemed genuinely upset that I had injured myself.

And there she is in this photo, standing almost to attention for my father as he takes his snap while the driver gets the car ready. It might be a weekend or holiday because we are not in school uniforms.

The car is shiny, indeed immaculate. I'm standing behind it in the driveway wearing a checked shirt and shorts.

My sister has on a little dress with braces and a white shirt, and is wearing a headband.

Next to us stands Ah Moy, the epitome of inscrutability. As I said, her face is familiar but it's the face of a stranger. A stranger who lived in our house for several years and managed to remain a mystery – a mystery that intrigues me now more than ever.

CHAPTER 6

UNCLE CYRIL

Some people yearn for their lost youth thinking of unrequited love or romantic adventures of the Huckleberry Finn variety. My Uncle Cyril's earliest and fondest memories always seemed to involve Chinese food. When we used to sit and reminisce about Hong Kong days, which we often did, he would get a faraway look in his eyes as he relished the recollection of some noodle dish of yore, a delicacy he had eaten at some *dai pai dong* (open-air food stall) back in 1947. He wasn't a literary person (like my father, Cyril was never to be seen reading a book) but the poetry that flowed during his remembrances of meals past was inspired. He would become quite florid and eloquently include all the colour of the scenery in which his noshing had occurred. The noodle dish at the apex of his culinary memories had been eaten while he sat on a small wooden stool in Kowloon City, which in the Forties was still a virtual remnant of the Qing Dynasty.

Cyril was the youngest of the four Brown brothers and the uncle I was closest to. I barely knew the others, Bob and Harold. He was also the one my father was closest to. He would often call me Cyril accidentally – which seemed habitual and affectionate – before correcting himself.

At times over the years Cyril was my father's right-hand man in the construction business which is why he came to join Dad in Hong Kong after we'd been there for eighteen months or so. With my father's business burgeoning in the bustle of 1960s Hong Kong – and his father having passed on – he needed help from someone he could trust. He had already parted ways with his Chinese partner, Tang, for reasons that remain unclear. So he called Cyril in Sydney who proved quite happy to come back to the place he regarded as his spiritual home. And there was always the food. So he, my Aunty Ruth and their three children – Michael and twins Veronica and Peter – moved back to the colony, setting in mid-Kowloon.

The other brothers stayed in Australia. Bob lived in Sydney with his wife, Maureen (a raven-haired woman who was part-Macanese) and their five children. In her younger years Aunty Maureen had been an exotic beauty. She and Bob, the eldest of the Brown brothers, married young in Hong Kong after meeting one day on the Star ferry. The cute little red-brick Rosary Catholic Church where they tied the knot is still there on Chatham Road South in Tsim Sha Tsui, one of those little survivors from the past that jostle with modern skyscrapers. Built in 1905, it's the oldest Catholic Church in Hong Kong. Jesuit-settled Macau can boast churches hundreds of years older.

The four brothers all worked for my grandfather in Hong Kong in the post-war years although work wasn't exactly Bob's forte according to my father. Bob was a lovely bloke but, as Dad would say, he couldn't work in an iron lung. And my old man reckoned he had never been the same after he was imprisoned by the Chinese in the 1950s. The sampan he was fishing from had apparently been blown into Chinese waters during a storm and, according to my father, the Communists 'brainwashed' him. Afterwards, on one of my father's building sites back in Australia, Bob was put in charge of a late shift. When Dad arrived to check on their progress one evening most of the men were standing around doing nothing.

My father asked a few of the men what was going on and each one said Bob had made him foreman. There were more foremen than workers which explains why nothing was happening. My father went looking for Bob and found him in the site shed eating toasted sandwiches and studying the form guide. Bob was a compulsive eater and also a bit of a gambling addict, and Hong Kong was a good place to indulge both compulsions. Bob apparently won quite often, successes mitigated by the fact that he had a tendency to bet on every horse in the race.

When my father went to see him about making most of the workforce into foremen, Dad started the conversation as he often did.

"You bloody idiot," he roared. What do you think you're doing? You can't make everyone foreman or nothing will get done."

Bob said he liked to reward good work with promotion and consequently had promoted most of the crew before retiring to the shed to eat yet another toasted sandwich and drink more coffee.

According to Dad, Bob not only had a sweet tooth, he was also (and I can relate to this foible) a career hypochondriac, always moaning and groaning about his latest ailment. Nothing was ever diagnosed. I remember him at family gatherings when we would come home from Hong Kong on holidays. He would be sitting in an armchair complaining about his stomach as a Chinese feast was being prepared in the kitchen by several aunts. Bob was no slouch as a Chinese chef himself – despite virtually claiming to have won World War II single-handed I suspect his war was actually spent as a cook in the Royal Air Force –and sometimes he would do the cooking too, then say he was too ill to eat it. This was rubbish because he was always the first at table and had a pretty healthy appetite for a bloke who claimed to be dying. My father accused him of eating like a gannet. After having his fill he would take to his armchair again to grumble about how indisposed he was. I must have been secretly taking notes, I think, or can hypochondria be genetic? When I'm well enough I fully intend to do some research on that.

The family theory was that Bob's stomach problem was caused by an intestinal blockage: some *cha sui bao* (pork bun) consumed aeons ago was stuck in there somewhere and causing all his problems, we reckoned.

Sporadic family gatherings were the only time I saw Bob so I didn't know him very well at all and most of what I knew was family legend transmitted by Dad through the prism of his self-confessed warped sense of humour.

I knew even less about Uncle Harold. The man who had carried my grandfather out of the POW camp when serving on the *Maidstone* was the black sheep of the family. He worked with the other brothers but was unreliable due to increasingly heavy drinking. Harold left the family company sometime in the 1950s and moved to Perth. Reports of him were few and far between but when we moved to Hong Kong my father used to get panicked phone calls from him, usually involving pleas for money. It was always urgent. In Perth Harold was working in the building industry and once rang saying he'd nearly lost an arm in a workplace accident and could money be sent immediately to cover his hospital bills. Turned out he'd basically nicked a finger: according to Harold he had almost severed his arm.

My old man usually wired the money. Harold died young from the ravages of alcoholism and I have no memories of him at all, but in recent years a son of his has made contact and shared photos of Harold with us. He was a good-looking bloke whose life was ruined by the grog.

Cyril, on the other hand, was abstemious and hard-working. He had only one vice: he and my Aunty Ruth smoked like chimneys. "If I could eat cigarettes, I would," he once told me when I enquired whether he'd ever considered quitting.

He had four stints in Hong Kong – as a child, as a young man, then in the Sixties when he worked for my father, and finally in the Eighties when he went back to work on the MTR for what was really the Browns' last stand, when it became clear that Hong Kong really was a borrowed place living on borrowed time. Cyril was the last of the dynasty to work in Hong Kong. Our very own Last Emperor.

In the Sixties Cyril and Ruth, along with my cousins, would join us for Sunday lunch after they had gone to Mass. We weren't churchgoers. My father was a lapsed Catholic, my mother an unconvinced Presbyterian. We went to Sunday school for a while in Hong Kong. That didn't last long, though.

Sometimes we kids all dressed up in little tailor-made suits for these family gatherings.

Despite the incessant smoking Cyril was pretty fit and in the Sixties he studied tae kwon do with a Korean master in Hong Kong and ended up a black belt, which impressed us. I used to love going round to their place because Cyril had a little tree stump set up in his tiny patch of yard. It had thick rope around it and he used it to condition his hands, pounding away at it hour after hour. My cousin Michael and I used to emulate him, scuffing our knuckles something horrible in the process.

I would run into Cyril at the various building sites Dad's company was working on. He and my father would often be in gumboots, sloshing around in the mud. While specialising in foundation work they also built public housing, new blocks of flats to house the refugees still pouring in from China and living in squatters' camps around the colony. They also built wharves. The construction work was all Greek to me, I had no understanding of the business – no feel for it at all – and site visits only left me confused, wondering how the hell they would ever get a building out of such a tangled mess of steel. My father and Cyril both spoke Cantonese which helped in their dealings with the workmen. Uncle Cyril's Cantonese was superior to Dad's. He was quite fluent in this colourful and expressive dialect with its Italian-style hand gestures. The Cantonese also have what you might call an affinity for profanity. Cyril could swear in Cantonese for up to an hour and still not run out of curses.

He worked with my father in Hong Kong for a few years until they fell out when my father said he wanted to move him to Manila. Dad was expanding the business there. He was in partnership with a fellow called Felipe Cruz (known, I believe, as F.F. Cruz) who was friendly with the new President, strongman Ferdinand Marcos, who was eventually deposed. In fact the old man once played golf with Cruz and Marcos. Most people remembered Marcos's wife, Imelda, better for her infamous shoe collection. Doing business in Asia five decades ago involved what we might now recognise as corruption. In the 1960s, though, business was business and having the imprimatur of the Philippines President didn't hurt.

Cyril wasn't at all keen on moving his family to Manila. He had been there to help set up the business and wasn't a big fan of the place. It was more unruly than Hong Kong. The first big job my father's company was doing there was in Iloilo province where the site had an armed guard unit in case of attack by local guerrillas. To us that sounded exciting. Not to Cyril.

In the end he simply refused to go and my father was so annoyed he said that if he didn't want to do as he was told he could finish up. So Cyril went back to Sydney and started in the house-building trade with my Aunty Kathleen's husband, John Wheeler, who had been one of Cyril's best mates in post-war Hong Kong. John, an Englishman who had grown up in Africa, had met the Browns on a slow boat to the colony from England after the war.

In contrast to John, who was never interested in coming back, Cyril loved Hong Kong and was sad to leave, yet again.

In Sydney he was a constant visitor to the restaurants in Dixon Street, Chinatown, where he would relive his glory days dish by dish.

So my father stayed on in Hong Kong without him.

When Wheeler was tragically killed in a car accident many years later Cyril decided he'd have another tilt at Hong Kong and applied for a job as a supervising engineer on the MTR, a project that would transform Hong Kong into one of the easiest metropolises in the world to get around. Aunty Ruth wasn't keen. She was born in Germany and her father had come out to work on the Snowy hydro scheme. She had the German love of order, and the chaos of Hong Kong never appealed to her as much as it did to Cyril. Yet she dutifully went with my uncle. By then they had another child, one of those surprises that sometimes come along when the other children are nearly grown-up. They named him David.

My cousin Veronica joined them in Hong Kong for a year or two before returning to Australia to live.

We were long settled back in Australia by the time Cyril and Ruth, with David in tow, were ensconced in a flat on busy Waterloo Road not far from Kowloon Hospital. In 1985 they invited me to go and stay with them and this was rather a momentous trip for me because it was my first time back to Hong Kong since leaving in late 1969.

At first I was almost reluctant to go because Hong Kong was preserved in the aspic of memory for me and had taken on the dimensions of a personal mythology I wanted to keep intact. What if reality failed to measure up to the myth?. Leaving Hong Kong so suddenly had been a wrench. During our years on the Gold Coast my 'lost world' had grown into the stuff of legend. My parents had been back only once, a trip I remember well because I was in my mid-teens and a mad surfer at the time. Not to mention a truant. An elderly couple they were friendly with were left to look after us while they were away and I took the opportunity to skip school for a few days and go surfing. Not sure how I got away with it. The suntan I had when my parents returned must have been a dead giveaway but nothing was ever said.

I guess it was a measure of how distracted we all were by our life and the inherent drama at the centre of it all swirling around my father's alcoholism. I understand it now for the disease it is but in those Gold Coast years it was a worm in the bud, the tragedy at the core of what should have been a happy family life back home in the Land of Oz.

Being the eldest son, I was at loggerheads with my father much of the time and his drinking drove us apart: it was an open sore that never healed. We were living in a big house by the river in a sunny place where everything was supposed to be fun, all of the time. But it wasn't.

Which is not to say we were always unhappy, only that Dad's drinking hung like a pall over the house and was starting to affect his health. When we moved to the Gold Coast he had tried his hand at a new venture, running a blue-metal quarry just outside what was then the little village of Nerang in the Gold Coast hinterland. I used to work there in my holidays driving trucks, smashing rocks and assisting the powder monkey, a taciturn fellow called Neil who wore an old German army helmet. How my mother, considering her nerves, allowed me to be involved with explosives I will never know.

Dad sold the quarry eventually to a bloke who happened to be a well-known crook. The fellow wouldn't pay up, sued my old man for misrepresentation and forced us to spend years in court trying to get the money back. The stress and expense eroded Dad's health and precipitated a slow decline, which was difficult for all of us.

My sister got married and had her own family to deal with, my brother became a bodybuilder and a Queensland cop. I went away to live in the country and write poetry, and ended up working on the local rag in the little Central Queensland town of Monto which, so the joke went, wasn't a bad little town as far as bad little towns go. Then I moved to the big smoke, Rockhampton, the place where I consider my career in journalism really began.

I came home to the Gold Coast intermittently and by then the big house had gone. My parents had downsized and moved closer to Broadbeach. On one visit home my father, who was grossly overweight and had developed diabetes, awoke with chest pains. I rushed into his bedroom when I heard my mother hysterical. We called an ambulance. I waited with him in his room as he gasped for breath and watched his life come to a relatively abrupt end there and then, on an otherwise ordinary spring morning in 1981 when everything should have been right with the world. He'd had a massive heart attack and nothing could be done. He was 55 years old.

I have tried to put that day out of my mind as the decades have worn on. People die, of course, but you hope they do so conveniently … in hospital or in a far-off city. The visceral experience of having my father die in front of me was harrowing beyond belief and the experience is like a scar on my psyche. I think it's no accident that my own drinking escalated after that wrench as I tried to numb the pain. In reality I think I was suffering from what would now be called post-traumatic stress disorder as well as a certain amount of guilt. Because there were times, when he was in his cups and the house was in emotional disarray, that I wished he was dead.

I have carried that with me for years and cried many tears for him but you can never shed enough, never find an end to the grief. So you live with it, somehow.

It was tough being the person who had to ring people and tell them Dad was gone. I called my Uncle Cyril in Hong Kong where he was working on the MTR construction project. He flew back for the funeral, and after watching the coffin slide away to be consumed by flames we stood outside, smoking cigarettes together, and he asked me if I would visit him and Aunty Ruth in Hong Kong. Of course I said I would.

It took me a few years to get there though. When I finally did it was with a mixture of excitement and misgiving. Luckily, I found that the visit didn't spoil my recollections at all and despite the many trips back since the old Hong Kong has remained preserved, like some archival footage untouched by the present and always there to refer to in the dusty recesses of my mental museum. I play it back regularly like an old movie, half forgotten, sometimes misremembered.

That first trip back to visit Cyril was momentous. I arrived at Kai Tak, the plane diving down and almost scraping the roofs of the concrete jumble they call Kowloon City, so close to the buildings that you could see people in their living rooms. Whenever we landed there as kids, my father claimed he had seen some bloke picking his nose. What we actually saw was mostly washing hanging from the apartment buildings, unless our approach was from the sea. Then it was a nerve-jangling descent onto that famous finger of a tarmac that stuck out into Kowloon Bay, making for one of the hairiest landings in the world.

I arrived in torrential summer rain. My uncle, reeking of English Blazer cologne, was there to meet me wearing his signature too-short shorts and one of those body shirts that accentuate both biceps and man boobs. My cousin David, then a young teenager, was with him. We drove through the neon city back to their little flat in Waterloo Road with the rain still pouring down in thick sheets. The driveway to their little compound had the usual ineffective boom gate staffed by a Chinese man who peered through the curtain of rain to verify that it was a resident returning.

The flat was small, comfy and freezing. Because we arrived in midsummer the air conditioning was ramped up and, with the humidity outside at 100 per cent and the rain bucketing down, the windows were all fogged up. It felt quite claustrophobic.

My room lacked any scenic vista. It looked out on the underbelly of a flyover that carried cars downtown above the clogged artery of Waterloo Rd. The loud hum of the air con blanketed the sounds of traffic. Later, sitting in the freezing living room sipping jasmine tea and eating sweet Chinese wafer biscuits, I felt perfectly at home.

The following day I began, somewhat tentatively, making the rounds of my old haunts on a sentimental journey into my Hong Kong childhood. My cousin, who was at my alma mater, King George V School (KGV), was on school holidays so he tagged along and I made him my official photographer. He could snap me in front of significant landmarks. There I am, standing outside the big iron gates of our house at 7 Devon Rd, Kowloon Tong. Now see me nearby in Kent Road Garden. One day we trudged to the top of Kadoorie Ave. which wasn't far from the flat although it was literally an uphill struggle in the humidity. It all seemed strange because at that time everything was still pretty much still there. One day we caught a taxi to Kowloon Junior School in Perth Street and it looked positively minuscule. Then we climbed the long stairway up to KGV and wandered the deserted grounds and quadrangles, running into the headmistress, Miss Smith, who was in her office despite its being the holidays. She seemed interested to have a past pupil visit and pulled out a copy of the school magazine, *The Lion*, in which she found a photo of me and my pals in the cricket team.

It was somewhat unreal to be back at KGV. Fifteen years may not seem all that long. Believe me, though, the length of my absence from Hong Kong felt like a gaping eternity. It was spooky walking around my old school with no one there, like stepping onto the deck of the *Mary Celeste*.

For dinner the first night of my visit, of course, followed family tradition by going to the KCC to feast on Singapore noodles.

Uncle Cyril was living out the Brown family's Hong Kong dream. With my father's death still fresh in our minds and hearts his presence there seemed like a kind of sacred duty, keeping the family flame lit in the colony that had meant so much to our dynasty down the decades. He was living the life Dad could no longer lead.

With his love of food, every evening was a culinary adventure played out at various Chinese restaurants around Kowloon. Once we dined at a local Mongkok eatery, Gum Yuen (Golden Circle), one of those places where the décor doesn't matter, the tables are bare and the waiters couldn't give a toss, basically throwing the food at you if you if you don't order what they suggest.

We had dinner there with a couple of Chinese blokes who used to work for my father – Yeung Bor Ke (known as Bor Jai) whose ruddy face with its broken blood vessels running away from his nose bespoke that love of brandy many Chinese seem to have. Bor Jai was famous in our family because of a story my father once told. On a family holiday home to Australia Dad bought Bor Jai, who had small children, a stuffed koala which he presented to him upon his return. A couple of days later Bor Jai came up to my father on site and said he had put the koala in a cage and tried feeding it rice but it was refusing to eat. Dad insisted the story was true.

The other diner there was Ngok Chen Sang, a Shanghainese who used to work for Dad, diving down into foundations filled with water or into the sea when they were building wharves. Dangerous work.

We talked of old times. They reminisced about my Dad and his capacity for food, drink and largesse. The Sixties, they intimated, had been their salad days. As we ate and drank, my uncle extolled the virtues of *chiu yim ha* (his favourite Cantonese prawn dish) which was a specialty of the house, along with the garoupa, which we didn't order, much to the waiter's dismay.

Cyril spent his life waxing eloquently about his last or his next Chinese meal. For breakfast, each morning of that first visit back, he insisted on walking me to a Mongkok street market where we bought such delicacies as congee (*juk* in Cantonese), a rice porridge with chicken or barbecued pork. We would buy fried breadsticks and dip them in the *juk*.

After breakfast my uncle would go off to work. He was in charge of the MTR's Shau Kei Wan section and one day I accompanied him on site. Shau Kei Wan is an underground station on the Hong Kong Island line heading east from Central and Admiralty. As it was being built, it looked to me like the scene of a small atomic explosion. It was one of those humid Hong Kong summer days when the sweat runs perpetually down the sides of your face. Wandering around brought back memories of childhood visits to equally chaotic building sites. We had lunch early at a hole-in-the-wall café not far from the site office. Seated on outside stools we feasted on noodles washed down with tall glasses of Carlsberg beer. I was still drinking back then. Soon afterwards it became clear to me – and everybody else, for that matter – that my relationship with alcohol was problematic. It took another five years for me to put the bottle down and I have lived a sober life ever since.

Next door was a coffin shop (there's a vast hillside necropolis close by Shau Kei Wan) and in front of the coffee shop sat a blind fortune-teller who based his predictions on the indentations found in the shells of small live terrapins, a local turtle-like reptile. He had a small basket of them from which he would pluck one out for his divining. Normally I would have had my fortune read too. This time, for some reason I held back. Who knows what I missed out on?

On my second last night in town I ventured out by myself, seized by a romantic notion of visiting the Foreign Correspondents Club, which John le Carré made famous in his novel *The Honourable Schoolboy*. I caught a taxi to the Star ferry and crossed the harbour to its counterpart on the island where I caught another cab from Admiralty to the club, on

Lower Albert Road, Central. My Australian press pass gained me entrée. I'm not sure what I was expecting (maybe le Carré's version). I just sat at the bar ignored by all and sundry as I chugged down over-sized glasses of Carlsberg and failed to make eye contact with anyone.

Later, and possibly because I was inebriated, I found myself back on Kowloon side in a place called Bar City where I drank more and waved away the bar girls who constantly approached me. This didn't go down well with the bouncers who ejected me onto the streets of Tsim Sha Tsui late in the evening. I caught a taxi back to Waterloo Rd and slept soundly with the air conditioner rattling way above me, blocking out the noise of the incessant traffic outside.

The next morning at breakfast my uncle's amah, Rose – traditional names seemed to be becoming a thing of the past – asked me about Australia and said she hoped one day to live there. I think she wanted my aunt and uncle to take her with them when they left.

Sad to say, these domestics – who become part of the family in their way – are basically abandoned when their European employers leave; and most of them are never heard of again.

Cyril drove me to the airport next day, reminding me en route about a dish of tiny dried fish he had meant to introduce me to but not got around to.

"Next time," I said, as one does.

After Hong Kong he moved on to Singapore to work on its MRT and eventually, rather bizarrely, retired to the small Victorian border town of Cobram, on the Murray River. When we lived in Melbourne in the early Nineties we used to visit him there. Luckily there was – as there always is – a Chinese restaurant in the town, where we supped and rekindled fond memories.

Cyril and Ruth had settled in Cobram because that was where my aunt's family settled after work on the Snowy Mountains scheme ceased in the 1950s. If you could find anywhere more different to Hong Kong than Cobram, well, good luck. Even as Uncle Cyril was physically in Cobram, his interior life was still based in Hong Kong where his main meal of the day was those noodles he ate back in childhood.

He died of cancer some years later and after his death my cousins Peter and David flew to Hong Kong on a mission. They had a pair of their father's cufflinks with them and, after eating their fill one day (both are self-confessed gourmands when it comes to Chinese food) they wandered along the boardwalk that fronts the harbour at Tsim Sha Tsui.

Not far from the Star ferry terminal they paused and dropped the cufflinks into the glassy green water.

My cousin recalled his father digging pottery and other trinkets out of the mud on building sites in Hong Kong. Cyril had cleaned them and created out of them a cabinet of curiosities. David and Peter had decided it was only fitting they leave behind something of Cyril's that would remain in Hong Kong forever.

The Brown family in Hong Kong in 1939 … back row Bob, Harold, my grandmother Christina May, Lord Roberts Brown, Christine …(front row) Kathleen, Eileen, Edward (Ted) and Cyril

My mother and Lai Wing-on on my parent's honeymoon

Me and my brother Stephen on our first rickshaw ride – Middle Road, Tsim Sha Tsui not long after our arrival in Hong Kong in 1963

A Sunday outing to the Castle Peak Hotel in 1964

Ah Moy, my sister and me as our driver gets the car ready for a jaunt

With my sister Jane at Tiger Balm Gardens circa 1965

Myself a mandarin … with my cat Kitty in the flat at Yau Yat Chuen

My glamorous mother Janet

My Uncle Cyril and Cousin Michael Brown

Pouting at lunch in the New Territories in 1968

Me, my brother and sister in the front garden at 7 Devon Road with Lion Rock in the background

At home in Yau Yat Chuen

The house at 7 Devon Road

Michael (left) and Rhett Hutchence watch my brother blowing out the candles on his birthday cake

My brother Stephen, Michael Hutchence and me on a sampan on our way to Hebe Haven

My mum and dad at a cocktail party in Hong Kong in the late 1960s

Tony Parr on one of my father's building sites

Dad, mum, my Aunty Ruth and Uncle Cyril on the front steps of the front porch at 7 Devon Road

My cricket team at King George V School in 1968. I'm third from the left in the back row

A typical Kowloon beach scene from my childhood

My spiritual home – photograph courtesy of The Peninsula Hong Kong

CHAPTER 7

NINE DRAGONS

Whenever we moved in Hong Kong it would always be from one Kowloon abode to another. We're Kowloon people, I can't say it any plainer than that. We have always been Kowloon people, and always will be. That peninsula on the southern tip of China, with its eight hills, is our world. It was my grandfather's world, my father's world and mine. It will always be home.

There are Kowloon people – and then there are those who live on the island, Hong Kong-side. They are worlds apart. Well, that may be an exaggeration: in truth they are just a short Star ferry ride away or one stop on the MTR. Even today people from Hong Kong side jokingly ask if they will need their passport to go to Kowloon.

For us Kowlooners Hong Kong side seems distant. When I was a boy we regarded people who lived there as, well, toffs. Anyone who lived up around The Peak was virtually an aristocrat. Anyone who lives there now is very likely a billionaire. Take a stroll around Governor's Walk, that lovely leafy path around The Peak not far from the famous Peak Tram terminus (now a multi-level mall), and you will see the sort of residences any warlord would be happy to inhabit.

Gweilos (the Cantonese slang term for Westerners which means, literally, 'ghost men') are to be found amid the crammed streets and apartment towers that make up what is known as Mid-Levels, a kind of First World ghetto where it seems most Westerners cluster.

When we stayed Hong Kong-side some years ago I felt like an interloper and was never quite at ease. That's not a new feeling.

Cities around the world are often divided in this way. The place I now call home is Brisbane and I live on the Northside. I have done so ever since arriving in 1986. Cross the river to the Southside and I am instantly lost. It's another world. So it is when I cross from Kowloon to the island.

In Hong Kong we usually stay Kowloon-side – for at least a few nights at The Peninsula, depending on our budget. We usually prefer to do The Pen at the end of our stay because I like to leave on a high. Last time we had to stay there for the first few days instead and then shift to a respectable enough nearby hotel. It seemed like an awful comedown in comparison. The folks at The Pen insisted on driving us there in one of the house Rolls-Royces so we rocked up like royalty. The small crowd that gathered to watch our arrival was pretty disappointed when we got out. I mean, who the hell are *we*?

I feel at home in Kowloon, like a tourist across the water. Once I had it in mind to visit the famous Luk U Tea House on Hong Kong side. It's on Stanley Street in Central and is cherished as the haunt of Cantonese opera and movie stars. It has that old-Shanghai feel with the wood panelling and all. I wanted to soak up that atmosphere, so late one morning we went by Star Ferry and walked from Admiralty to the historic teahouse.

The waiters there were diffident, to say the least, and would have turned us away if they could have, I'm sure. When they spotted my backpack they turned their noses up and grudgingly led us to a small table near the kitchen door. The worst table in the restaurant, as it turned out, even though the establishment was nearly empty.

"Can't we sit at one of those tables over there?" I asked.

"No," the waiter said gruffly. "They are reserved for customers."

"What are we, chopped liver?" I muttered under my breath.

They virtually chucked the food at us when it came and then fawned over other people who had begun arriving – obviously regular customers, who were all treated like minor royals.

I asked to see the manager to complain about our table and the service, only to be told he wasn't in. In fact I was pretty sure he was standing nearby being obsequious but I let it go.

We then made to leave and that elicited slightly more enthusiasm from the staff as they showed us the door. It felt as if we were being ejected after a very unsatisfactory 45 minutes of being ignored by the rudest waiters on the planet.

"Now you see, that wouldn't happen in Kowloon," I said as we chugged back across the harbour.

Kowloon is the anglicised name of the place. In Cantonese it's *Gauluhng* which means Nine Dragons. In Chinese mythology a dragon resides in every hill. What's odd is that the district has only eight hills – Kowloon Peak, Tung Shan,

Tate's Cairn, Temple Hill, Unicorn Ridge, Lion Rock, Beacon Hill and Crow's Nest.

The ninth dragon was not a hill at all but, rather, an Emperor – a boy Emperor, Bing, whose doomed court fled to the area during the Sung Dynasty. The story goes that he counted eight hills in the region and decided to name the area Eight Dragons (it doesn't have the same ring, does it!) until a courtier reminded him that, being an Emperor, he was also counted as a dragon and so it became Nine Dragons.

It is an historical fact that the Emperor's court did reside there so it's conceivable the story is true. I hope it is.

The Kowloon Peninsula is presided over by Lion Rock, which features what looks like a seated lion at the summit of that dignified peak. This lion looks out across the peninsula over Beacon Hill, to the gracious garden suburb of Kowloon Tong below, where we lived for several years with a view of the majestic beast mountain from our front yard.

The lion can even 'see' as far as tourist-infested Tsim Sha Tsui where Kowloon bumps up against Victoria Harbour in a precinct crowned by The Peninsula. Nowadays the Kowloon waterfront esplanade, which edges around the harbour, is a popular recreational area. Of an evening, people throng to the nightly laser light shows Hong Kong puts on for visitors and locals alike. The views from Kowloon are stunning, much better than those from Hong Kong side. From Kowloon you get a sweeping view of the island's glittering towers all lit up and sparkling, a neon wonderland every night of the year.

In early colonial times Kowloon was regarded as a backwater, a den of iniquity for the lower classes where thieves congregated. It was famous for the notorious Walled City, a relic of the fabled past that survived until 1994 when it was demolished and replaced by a little park and a community centre. In my boyhood that place, not very far from where we lived, was a forbidden world reputedly ruled by Triads, riddled with opium dens (or so they said), a netherworld of Old China. The Walled City was the badlands, as was Kowloon itself.

The British civil servants, the toffs and taipans, all lived on Hong Kong side and looked down at Kowloon from their houses on The Peak. When they built The Peninsula on Kowloon side there was amazement and it was predicted the hotel would be a white elephant. Who would want to stay in Kowloon?

But it made sense with the railway that connected China with Hong Kong running all the way to the nearby Star ferry terminal; and passengers from the ocean liners berthed at the old Kowloon Wharf could just trot across the road to their plush lodgings.

The Browns having settled in Kowloon in the late Thirties and returned there after the war, there was never any question of us living anywhere else in the Sixties.

Kowloon was my patch, my playground, as a kid and we ranged freely around Tsim Sha Tsui. The last section of Nathan Road, the main artery leading to the harbourfront, is known as the Golden Mile, at night a glittering Vegas-like strip; by day a busy shopping precinct pitted with hotels, malls, high-end retail outlets and restaurants. Navigating the last couple of blocks is sometimes a trial as you dodge the touts trying to sell you fake Rolexes and lure you into nearby tailor's shops. Still, I love it.

The streets around here are my streets … Kimberley Road,

Granville Road, Mody Road, Humphreys Ave., Hankow, Haiphong and Cameron Roads. Blindfold me and send me down Nathan Rd and I will find all these thoroughfares quite easily. Mum used to take us shopping for cheap clothes in Granville Rd back in the Sixties, my pal Greg England lived in a penthouse on the Cameron Rd corner, my record store was in Mody Rd and, as previously described, the Swindon Book Co. on Lock Rd is a great survivor. I return to these streets whenever I am back in town and, though much has changed, the geography remains unaltered and now Kowloon Park is a green haven in the middle of it all.

Kowloon feels more relaxed to me than Hong Kong side. The financial heart is still Central where glittering towers soar into the heavens, although Kowloon now has its own financial skyscraper, the soaring 118-storey International Commerce Centre, a phallic statement that dominates West Kowloon. There never was a West Kowloon when I was growing up: it's one of those new precincts created by reclamation. Kowloon grows every year as they tack on more land and the harbour seems to get narrower and narrower, making the water slop from side to side as in a bathtub.

While Central is a sea of pinstripe suits Tsim Sha Tsui is more casual and, it must be said, more of a tourist trap. Yet I feel at home there and, for all its changes, some things remain the same. Chungking Mansions, for example.

This tatty yet venerable high-rise labyrinth of guest houses in the middle of downtown Nathan Rd is a residual symbol of Hong Kong in the Sixties, a remnant of the past that stubbornly squats amongst the expensive gold and jewellery stores, hotels and shopping malls of downtown Kowloon.

Even as a kid I was fascinated by Chungking Mansions. Built in 1961 it already had a reputation as a no-go zone by the time we arrived. It was, and still is, where people who can't afford to stay in hotels prop when they are in Hong Kong. Traders from Africa and the subcontinent gathered there then and still do today. Wander down the right-hand side of Nathan Rd from the harbourfront and you will soon come across Chungking Mansions. You will know it at once by the crowd on the pavement outside … Africans in colourful traditional garb, men from India, Pakistan and elsewhere all wheeling and dealing on the footpath. Money changers occupy the mouth of the arcade that leads to the lifts here, which always have queues that stream back out onto the street. Being claustrophobic, I could never enter one of these slim elevators and the idea of staying there has never dawned on me.

That has been hammered into me since I was a boy. My mother always used to turn her nose up as we passed and gave the place a wide berth on the pavement to get away from the "types" who still crowd the pavement today.

The Brisbane writer Hugh Lunn confessed to me one day that as a young journo on a tight budget he had stayed there and he wrote about that in his book *Spies Like Us*. "I rented a room off a Filipino trumpeter," he tells me. In his book he writes '… I could see immediately why the owners had found it necessary to call the building a "mansion". The concrete exterior was filthy and the interior totally rundown.' I know of only one other *gweilo* who has dossed there. Call it colonial snobbery but there you have it.

Increasingly over the years I have developed a fascination with the place and we have begun to make forays into the building, wandering the ground-level arcades with their cheap grocery stores and excellent curry joints.

Once, when we were staying at The Pen and trying to massage our budget, I went across the road to Chungking Mansions to buy dinner and furtively ferried it back to our deluxe hotel, trying not to be too obvious with my plastic bags and containers smelling of curry as I navigated the foyer and hurried past reception.

We often eat there now when we're in town but I have still never ventured beyond the ground floor despite being encouraged to do so by wiry young South Asians in black trousers and plain white shirts who press flyers into your hand as you pass in an attempt to lure you to their upstairs restaurants.

Last time we were in the colony someone from the Royal Geographic Society was giving a public lecture on Chungking Mansions. It's quite the sociological phenomenon apparently. There is even a book about the joint – *Ghetto at the Center of the World* by Gordon Mathews – and it has been celebrated on the big screen in Wong Kar-wai's 1994 movie *Chungking Express*. It also features in Michael Connelly's book *Nine Dragons* in which he describes it as a 'post-modern Casablanca' which sounds about right.

Its very existence seems to defy modern Hong Kong, this 17-storey anomaly in the middle of modern Tsim Sha Tsui.

I happen to love TST, as we sometimes call it, yet Kowloon is so much more than Tsim Sha Tsui. We seldom went much beyond TST as children but now I love to wander further into the bustling heart of the peninsula, to Yau Ma Tei and the jade market,– always worth a visit even though you have to run the gauntlet of the stallholders there.

Yau Ma Tei sits between Tsim Sha Tsui and Mongkok. Mongkok was mostly off limits to us as children although my father had his first office around there. However, I remember strictly regulated visits with my mother steering us through streets that looked like old movie sets. Hawkers passed by with baskets on yokes across their shoulders, rickshaws carried customers along the streets as women carried babies in slings on their backs, the bubs' heads lolling like rag dolls'. Beggars held out their bowls as we passed and children approached, claiming to be orphans. "No mama, no papa, no whisky soda" was a popular old refrain heard on the streets, traceable to some visiting GI in days long gone.

Mongkok is still redolent of old Hong Kong although it is changing.

We stayed in Mongkok on a visit when my son was small, stopping at what was then the Langham Place Hotel, now luxurious Cordis Hotel on Shanghai St. The neighbouring streets abound with food stalls and cafés, markets and malls where you go shoulder to shoulder with the locals, and all night every night the glare of neon signs is reflected off clouds that hang low in the monsoon season.

The juxtaposition of Western modernity and the traditional Orient is starker here than anywhere in Hong Kong. Here beats the Chinese heart of Kowloon.

The quarter to the west of the hotel was once the waterfront, although with reclamations the water is now further away and port facilities have expanded this part of Kowloon. A vestige of the old bustling waterfront precinct lives on … a wet market, one of those places that seem to have circumvented regulation and the dawning of the 21st century. Here dying fish look up at you with sad eyes as they are laid out on racks for sale, where bags of frogs writhe like visions of hell from some Hieronymus Bosch painting, while buckets of live prawns and mussels await their fate on a plate.

When we stayed at the Langham Place we went for a walk through this wet market, marvelling yet horrified.

We paused at one stall to watch a butcher sharpen his cleaver before chopping up a stingray he had laid out on a board in front of him. A cigarette hanging from his lower lip spilt ash onto the board. On this excruciatingly muggy morning he had his singlet rolled up in an attempt to keep cool. Sweat rolled down his face and dripped onto his exposed belly.

He wouldn't have passed workplace health-and-safety muster in Australia but, undaunted in this other world, he began hacking into the stingray as he puffed away on his fag. When he was done he laid out its remains in front of his stall along with evidence of the other atrocities he had committed that morning. One of the things I love about Hong Kong is that, despite living at technology's leading edge, the old analogue Hong Kong is still within reach, easily discoverable amongst the dying fish mouths of Mongkok.

Being an unreconstructed Hong Kong tragic it seemed important early on in my relationship with my future wife to ascertain whether she would be Honkers-friendly – and, more to the point, would she like Kowloon? She had never been there before and chances were if we stayed together we would be spending quite a bit of time there. I felt sure she *would* like it. I mean, who doesn't love Kowloon? Even so …

I remember, one day years ago, running into a fellow I

know in Brisbane who had just returned from the territory, where he stayed up by the Kowloon waterfront.

"Hong Kong is so boring," he told me. "There's nothing to do. What can you do there?"

I look at him, mouth agape, wondering – can he possibly be serious? What if my prospective bride felt the same? Was that conceivable?

There was only one way to find out.

Our first trip there was in late 1991 not long after Sandra and I had started living together. It was our first overseas trip, an epic journey beginning with a few days in Thailand where we inhabited a fleapit in a *soi* off Sukhumvit Road.

Then we flew to Kathmandu, our base for a month in Nepal. My wife had friends living in a house in Maharajgunj, a suburb close to the heart of the capital.

Off we went trekking in the high Himalayas, a twelve-day slog up and down the Langtang Valley. The first stage was a six-hour ordeal from Kathmandu along a dirt road in a car that you wouldn't have wanted to drive around the block in. The trek was amazing and exhausting, and the profanities I uttered trudging up and down those hills are probably still echoing across the valleys.

After Nepal we went to Hong Kong. This was to be the litmus test and I had fixed on the idea of proposing to Sandra there for sentimental reasons.

We flew from the Nepalese capital with Royal Nepal Airlines, an outfit I wasn't familiar with and was a bit nervous about. You had to wonder, if they couldn't manage to get the airport toilets to flush properly, how they could run an airline?

There was an awfully awkward moment when all the

passengers rushed from one side of the plane to the other to view the Himalayas and I screamed out: "Sit down, you idiots, you'll tip the plane!" The steward explained to me in no uncertain terms that this was not possible.

The flight path from Kathmandu to Hong Kong I call the Gurkha Route because a battalion of Nepalese Gurkha troops were stationed in Honkers in the twilight of the British colonial era. There is still plenty of traffic between the two destinations today. Many Gurkhas and their families stayed on after the handover and now work in security and other occupations.

Thankfully our Royal Nepal Airlines flight made it. As we made our way through Customs I watched the two young Nepalese men ahead of us get the once-over. They had bags containing Buddha statues and they were obviously suspected by the officers of smuggling drugs in them, so the Buddhas were dismantled with screwdrivers and knives while the young guys stood nervously by.

We caught a taxi from Kai Tak to our digs, Park Hotel on the corner of Cameron Road and Chatham Road South. The hotel has been refurbished in recent years and looks quite nice now. Back in 1991 it was a touch shabby and at that time we were too poor to afford The Pen.

I had booked the Park because it was connected to my childhood when I suppose it was relatively new. For some reason it was popular with Aussies.

We spent a couple of nights there when we were migrating back to Australia and had moved out of our mansion in Kowloon Tong.

It wasn't exactly The Ritz. Still, I like that end of Cameron

Rd and its proximity to Hau Fook Street, a pedestrian cul-de-sac devoted to food, with hotpot a speciality. Easy access to Hau Fook is gained via a lane that runs from Cameron Rd not far from the Park.

On our first morning together in Hong Kong we eschewed the Park's breakfast for French toast and coffee at The Pen and there's a photo of me sitting there looking smug with the early light streaming in. I look a bit like Bob Geldof – the hair and the emaciation, you understand. I believe 'elegantly wasted' is the correct term.

We wandered the streets of Kowloon and I was rather pleased that Sandra seemed to like the joint. Our first night we ate in Hau Fook St.; on the second we treated ourselves to Peking duck at an upstairs restaurant in nearby Granville Rd. I always like the idea of Peking duck but it's awfully fatty and I was up all night clearing my throat.

It was apparent to me that Sandra had taken to Hong Kong, and it was an especially good idea to come here following Nepal. After the rigours of trekking, this seemed like the lap of luxury. Now all I had to do was to pop the question.

One evening, after an early dinner, we were reclining in our slightly tatty room watching a movie (*A Handful of Dust*, starring Rupert Graves and Kristin Scott Thomas) when, out of the blue as it must have seemed – it certainly did to me – I asked if she would marry me.

Not exactly down on one knee and maybe not the most romantic moment. But it worked. Sandra said yes, poor girl.

Predictably, I had forgotten something. The engagement ring.

"Wait a minute, there's that nice jewellery store next door,"

I recalled. It was still early and the shops were open so we went down into Cameron Rd.

The boutique in question had a respectable range of rings and eventually Sandra chose one she liked, which featured a rather fetching emerald. The burglars who fetched it from our house in Brisbane some years ago also seemed to like it. This was a good choice, according to the proprietor, even if I had a feeling any choice would have been good in his eyes. We were the only ones in the shop. He was red-faced and smelt of brandy, a popular tipple in Hong Kong. At one time this was the biggest market in the world for cognac. On a little table behind the counter I noticed a glass containing a liquid the colour of tea – except that it wasn't tea. And he was obviously half cut.

As Sandra tried on her ring, the jeweller – oddly enough – was admiring my gold signet ring. When he asked to look at it I had to explain that I couldn't get it off. With all the travel and in Hong Kong's high humidity my pinkie had swollen up.

"Please, look at me," he said. He fixed me with a stare. "Hold hand out. Look at me please."

I humoured him. "OK," I said gingerly. Sandra looked askance.

The shopkeeper fixed me with a weird stare, I held out my hand and he slid the ring off my finger with ease.

"How did you do that?" I asked. He smiled inscrutably.

Then he picked up the emerald engagement ring Sandra had just taken off her finger.

"You buy?" he asked, rather too insistently. Sandra nodded.

"I buy," I said. He then told me the price and my heart sank. "Oh, right," I said. "Not sure if I have that much on me." My reserves were low.

"Don't worry, we can put it on my credit card," Sandra said. Start as you mean to go on, they say.

No matter. I may have been skint but we were in Kowloon and, better still, we were engaged. As if to prove it, Sandra had a ring on her finger so we went back to our room and celebrated with tea and digestive biscuits. Luxury.

CHAPTER 8

THE INSCRUTABLE MR LAI

In the middle of 1964, after a short time at La Salle Road, we shifted house again in Kowloon, across Waterloo Rd to Yau Yat Chuen – just a short hop really. We moved into a first-floor flat at 4 Wistaria Rd, a floral address in a floral suburb. All the names in Yau Yat Chuen relate to flowers.

As well as Wistaria Rd there are Begonia, Dianthus, Peony and Marigold Roads and so on. Cute. The suburb's name means 'one more village', the final line of a work by the poet Lu Yu that was commonly taught in the territory's Chinese schools.

This was an enclave for the well-heeled, with large houses and spacious apartment buildings. Now, when many of the bigger houses there have been divided into multiple residences, things are packed in a bit tighter; back in the Sixties it was relatively genteel, a little idyll in the midst of bustling Kowloon. On the hillsides not that far from us, squatters who had come south to seek refuge from the Communists across the border were living in squalor as they waited for the public housing that was being built to accommodate them, housing that in some case was being built by my father's construction firm.

Close by, life was a struggle in teeming Mongkok.

If a neighbourhood could be said to live in a state of denial, Yau Yat Chuen was that neighbourhood – quiet, possessed of a gracious lifestyle and clean streets lined with largely empty houses and flats invisible behind high walls.

The first thing I remember about Yau Yat Chuen had nothing to do with its geography or character, however. I remember it as the site of an epiphany, if you can call a negative experience an epiphany. The flat at 4 Wistaria Rd was where I first encountered anxiety. Maybe I had a free-floating and subtle form of it before we moved there and it's hard to know exactly how that developed. The restlessness and peripatetic nature of my early life may have been part of the cause. Unless it was genetic. Certainly my mother was always highly strung and, being the eldest and rather bookish, I was close to her. My father was a tough guy and I loved him very much: the truth is, we didn't have a lot in common. As I've already said, so far as I know he never read a book. My mother was a little over-protective and one of my aunts dubbed me "the sensitive one". I'm not sure I was really all that sensitive; anxious, certainly.

Angst made its major debut a few months after we settled at Yau Yat Chuen. It happened like this: one night I began to fear that my parents, who were out for the evening, might not come home. Their social life got busier and busier the longer we were in Hong Kong. There was an endless round of cocktail parties, dinners and functions at various embassies, the Australian High Commission or The Peninsula. Increasingly we kids were left at home with Ah Moy. That's the handy thing about having an amah: you have a ready-made live-in babysitter.

This night I was lying in bed, unable to go to sleep as I

listened for my parents to arrive home. The front door opening and closing would be proof of life and then I could go off to sleep. As they were later than usual I went out into the lounge room which glowed with the lights from our fish tank where guppies, neon tetras and a lone Siamese fighting fish floated aimlessly through the days and nights.

I went over to the heavy curtains, opened them and looked out at the street. Our driver tended not to work in the evenings so Mum and Dad would probably be coming in a taxi, although occasionally some toffee-nosed friend would drop them in a chauffeur-driven limo. A couple of cabs drove along the street as I watched but they didn't stop. I stood there in my pyjamas, watching, waiting and becoming more anxious by the minute as my mind raced.

I imagined that something had happened to them, that there had been an accident on the way home or something equally catastrophic. I worked myself into quite a lather and began sobbing. Ah Moy, who had retired to her room at the end of the hall and was listening to the radio (the caterwauling of Cantonese opera emanated from within), must have sensed something was wrong. I'm not sure she could have heard anything over her radio but she came out into the living room and saw me standing there with tears streaming down my cheeks.

She seemed to understand in an instant why I was upset. "No cry, little master," she said. "No cry. Master and Missy home soon. You go bed."

With these words of comfort she escorted me back to the bedroom. I hadn't experienced tenderness from her before. It was the most private moment we ever experienced together.

Mostly she was efficient and distant, which I now see was her way of dealing with having to be constantly subservient.

That was the only really personal exchange with her that I can recall even though she lived with us for several years. My parents arrived home soon afterwards and I think she must have told them what was wrong because they came into my room, my father smelling of Old Spice and whisky, Mum wafting 4711-brand eau de cologne.

My father said I'd been silly while my mother suggested he leave things to her. She said it was all right, I shouldn't get upset. I felt ashamed. It was a panic attack, I guess, and it wouldn't be the last. And that's where it all started, in Yau Yat Chuen. People remember places for all sorts of reasons – for me that middle-upper-class Hong Kong oasis will always be synonymous with a deep and abiding existential anxiety.

Our flat there was reasonably expansive, certainly bigger than the little place at La Salle Rd. There was a small concrete balcony off the living room with a view over the leafy street. Soon after moving in we acquired a dog, a bitser called Sandy, the colour of a golden Labrador. It didn't seem very practical to have an animal in the flat but my father always had dogs and, after all, the amah could look after it.

The kitchen was spacious and a servery gave onto the dining area.

Besides anxiety my next strong Yau Yat Chuen memory is the smell of incense. Behind the apartment block was a small shrine where the amahs, cook boys and other staff burnt their joss sticks. It was a Taoist shrine (I'm not sure to which god or gods it was dedicated). Its centrepiece was a statuette inside a kind of painted box resting on a stand.

Occasionally I would see Ah Moy down there lighting her joss sticks, which gave off a slightly acrid incense familiar to anyone who lived in Hong Kong at that time. Once lit, the sticks would be proffered prayerfully with attendant bowing.

I loved to watch this ritual and sometimes lingered to watch the yellow sticks burn down. We used joss sticks to light fireworks which may have been sacrilegious but it was effective.

Sometimes, as well as the joss sticks, there were offerings of fruit and other food.

We were slowly becoming aware of this parallel world of Chinese customs existing alongside our rather secular Western lives.

My family was not at all religious. My mother, the nominal Presbyterian, took us to Sunday school when we first went to Hong Kong but that didn't last long. My father ascribed his lapsed-Catholic status to the brothers at La Salle College who, he said, had beaten the religion out of him. For all that, I think he always remained a believer. Not that he was bothered about our being baptised as Protestants. Neither of my parents seemed to have deep religious tendencies. Business, food and drink were the real objects of my father's devotions.

Neither of my parents seemed to pay much attention to the exotic world of Chinese spirituality that was all around us, if largely opaque.

I think I was more interested than anyone in what was going on out back of the flats. Standing there watching Ah Moy with her joss sticks and her mysterious deities was fascinating. And I loved the Chinese festivals … the annual Hungry Ghost Festival, Yulan, a kind of Chinese Halloween when restless spirits roam the earth. During the festival –

intrinsically linked to ancestor worship – offerings are made to spirits and ancestors. Bonfires are lit and *faux* money, known as Hell Banknotes, are burnt to offer financial help to those in another realm. My mother used to frown on the wasted food that was left out each year, rotting where it lay while the ghosts supposedly supped on it.

Not long after that festival came the Mid-Autumn or Moon Festival, an excuse for eating moon cakes and worshipping the full Moon. Pretty pagan really. The year was punctuated by these and other festivals, which mostly mystified us. The melange of Taoism and Buddhism practised in Hong Kong has always attracted me, though, and my love of incense has remained. I burn some every day in a small brazier I have at home.

Although we weren't religious quite a few of my friends from school were. There were a lot of European and American missionaries in Hong Kong in those days and we had joined the YMCA, which was quite evangelical in its way. Some of my friends' parents were missionaries, including those of my Australian mate Tim Budge (we're still friends all these decades later) and I knew a few Americans whose folks were also engaged in turning the heathen Chinese away from their gods, shrines and joss sticks – with but limited success.

By now I was settling into life in Kowloon and doing well at KJS. And I was reading voraciously. It was all Enid Blyton to begin with (her *Famous Five* and *Secret Seven* books) until I moved onto the Hardy Boys mysteries and then Rider Haggard, R.M. Ballantyne and Robert Louis Stevenson. While Dad thought reading a waste of time, Mum used to take me downtown to Swindon to feed my habit.

I had a growing circle of friends and a mate who lived nearby, Lawrence Tedd. His parents were friends with mine. The Tedds, who were from New Zealand, lived on the corner of Begonia and Wistaria Roads. Bob Tedd was some kind of bigwig with Air New Zealand and, like my father, a veteran of World War II. They used to attend the Dawn Service together, an Anzac tradition that was celebrated in Hong Kong which has had a large Australian community for decades. I remember them coming home one Dawn Service to our flat in Yau Yat Chuen. It was only mid-morning but they were obviously drunk.

Bob and his wife, Joan, had two children – Lawrence and Linda. Lawrence and I used to prowl the neighbourhood together. Hong Kong was deemed safe enough for kids to do that unsupervised. We used – or abused – our relative freedom to cause whatever mischief we could manage and that might mean pinching something from a local shop or setting off firecrackers and throwing cherry bombs, that sort of harmless fun. We also bought stink bombs, little glass capsules that, when crushed, stank like rotten eggs.

One day we were passing a dry cleaner's van that had its back doors open. The delivery man was inside a residence delivering so we thought it would be fun to place a couple of stink bombs inside the back of his truck and crush them. Which we did – and then ran for our lives. Our parents had no idea what we were up to, of course.

At the Tedds' place I hung out with them in their backyard. It was a jungly joint with a tall stand of bamboo and a stone stairway leading down to a pond on the lower level. In it were local pond terrapins and one day we found one of them floating dead so we decided to bury it in the backyard. We held a funeral service and played one of those little battery-powered toy organs to accompany the burial rite.

Sometimes we were unchaperoned with just their amah in charge, and she wasn't bothered with us at all. In secret Lawrence would take me up to his father's bedroom and show me the magazines his dad kept stashed in a cupboard. There were copies of *Playboy* and other girlie magazines, as they were known back then. You know, the sort that people always used to say they bought for the articles.

We were fascinated by the photos of naked women that were probably pretty tame. Still, this was forbidden fruit, which made it all the tastier.

While I'm not sure who came up with the idea to pinch some of the mags we decided Lawrence's father had so many that he wouldn't notice if a few went missing. And here's where it gets interesting: the plan was to take our haul to KJS and sell them to fellow students to make money to buy more stink bombs. Genius.

The plan came unstuck when the magazines were discovered in my school bag. My mother opened it to put my lunch in and got the shock of her life. I saw this unfolding in slow motion and rushed over in a bid to stop her – too late.

"Phillip, what is this?" she asked. If she didn't know I really couldn't tell her. I went red and she got a bit angry and asked where I had got the magazines from. I spilt my guts. Mum called Joan Tedd to tell her what she had found. I don't remember the conversation but do remember one word from it quite clearly. "Titties." She said it a couple of times. I got a bollocking over that and imagine that at the other end of the street Lawrence was getting a similar bollocking. How did we think, for one moment, that we would get away with a crazy scheme like that? Still, we were quite entrepreneurial in our way.

The Tedds sometimes visited our flat and on one of these visits Linda Tedd stood on our dog Sandy's tail when it was sleeping in the hallway. The dog woke in fright, jumped up and bit her on the face. It was a major disaster. Ah Moy came running and, when she saw what had happened, started wailing, "*Aiyah! Aiyah!*" The mothers screamed and pandemonium reigned. Of course the dog had to go and despite our protests my father had Sandy put down. The incident left a pall of grief hanging over the flat for weeks.

Not long after that incident I was outside the flats one day lurking in the street, as I did, when I found a kitten lying in the gutter. It was barely alive and its back legs didn't seem to be functioning at all but it was breathing. I picked it up, cradled it in my arms and took it upstairs. My parents were home, sitting in the living room listening to a Kingston Trio record on our Grundig radiogram, one of those old hi-fis that was part record player, part radio and part sideboard.

My father didn't like cats and suggested I go and put it back in the gutter where I'd found it, which seemed cruel. My mother suggested we keep it until it got better and then find a home for it. I had other ideas. So we nursed it, fed it milk, sardines and little titbits of rice (Ah Moy's suggestion because to the Chinese rice is the foundation of everything); and soon the cat was well again and walking around, quite happy with itself and its new home.

I called the kitten Kitty, which I confess wasn't particularly imaginative. It started sleeping on my bed and soon it became apparent that it was pretty well my cat. It followed me around and may have been grateful since I was the one who had picked it out of the gutter and given it this new life.

Kitty was my companion every night for the rest of our years in Hong Kong and I have this rather amusing photo of me looking like some kind of mini-mandarin with nerdy glasses, sitting in an armchair wearing a Chinese gown with a book beside me and Kitty adorning the headrest.

One day I came home from school to find my father sitting at our dining room table with a Chinese man. It was unusual to see Dad home at that time of day. On this occasion he was going away somewhere and he and Lai Wing-on – who we knew simply as Mr Lai – were going through some details about his trip.

On seeing me, Mr Lai smiled sweetly.

Mr Lai was one of the first Chinese people we met after arriving in Hong Kong. He worked for Dad although I was never quite sure what he did. A bit of everything, I think. He was some sort of office manager and general procurer. A small man with a birdlike countenance, he always had a smile lingering at the corners of his mouth. He was quiet and deferential, yet in his own way insistent. We had met him at my father's office a few times. He seemed very nice and unobtrusive; the sort of person who would surprise you by turning up right behind you just before you were about to summon him, as if he'd foreseen your need.

He seemed very happy to have my father back in Hong Kong. Mr Lai had worked for the family forever – right back to when he was a young man before World War II. He worked for China Construction Co. in the post-war years too, and was what colonialists used to term a family retainer. According to my mother he was devastated when the Browns left Hong Kong for Australia in the early 1950s. Hong Kong was like that, though: people would come and go, often never to be seen or heard of again. Servants, employees, friends, pets … all would be left behind when people returned to whatever they thought of as their Mother Country.

Mr Lai seemed to have spent a lot of his time waiting for the Browns to return. He was apparently overjoyed when my parents got married and came to Hong Kong on their honeymoon. According to Mum the honeymoon took forever. My parents were married in Sydney in late 1955 and then flew to Singapore, which back then was a long flight with stops for refuelling. My mother says when they touched down in Indonesia the people there were very rude to them, and she had a lifelong resentment against them.

When Mum and Dad finally made it to Hong Kong Mr Lai was waiting to welcome them with open arms. Well, maybe not open arms: he was a bit more restrained than that, in the Oriental fashion. He would never have shown that much enthusiasm openly. The joy he felt would probably have been reflected in his face. His eyes. Kind eyes.

I have a lovely black-and-white photograph from my parents' honeymoon and it tells a funny story. It was taken in a Chinese temple, possibly Man Mo – one of the territory's most famous Taoist temples – on Hollywood Road, Hong Kong Island. My mother is wearing an overcoat and scarf. It was December, after all, and winter can be quite bitter in Hong Kong, mainly in the early morning. In the photo my mother is standing, all rugged up, at the altar of this temple, behind her a large incense burner and beyond that assorted gods in their little pantheon. Bearing in mind that this was her honeymoon, the figure posing with her should, ostensibly, be my father.

It's not him. It's Lai Wing-on, looking quite pleased with himself, a rather quizzical look on his face. He was a touch shorter than my mother (and she wasn't tall). In the photo he's wearing an overcoat too, and what's left of his thinning hair appears to have been plastered to his head with hair oil. He was still using it in the Sixties and by then he didn't need any. Why bother when you have barely a dozen strands left up there?

Since my mother is in the shot with Mr Lai, I figure my father must have been busy taking the photo. He always was a happy snapper. Whatever the explanation, I have no photos of my father and mother on their honeymoon.

Mum once told me that Mr Lai was like their shadow the whole time. He was there to meet them at the airport, went with them to the hotel, saw to it that they checked in OK. And each morning he would wait in The Peninsula lobby until they came down, ready to spend another day with them. Mum was too polite to say anything and Dad didn't want anyone to lose face so Mr Lai escorted the happy couple all around Kowloon and the island.

Presumably he would have hinted to my father that he should come back to Hong Kong where he would be ready and waiting to serve them. When they left he was bereft.

Mr Lai had to wait until 1963 for my father's return. Looking at that photo from 1955 and comparing it with my memories of him in the Sixties I'm struck by one thing. He looked exactly the same. Some people reach a certain age and keep looking the same age until they hit their dotage. I reckon Mr Lai probably looked fifty when he was thirty, and still looked fifty at seventy. I don't know how old he was when I was a boy but he must have been getting on.

Still, he seemed kind of youthful and was always immaculate in sharpish suits and ties and that natty overcoat he was wearing in the photo.

My mother always spoke fondly of Mr Lai even if, like so many others of our acquaintance in Hong Kong, he remained mysterious and unknowable, part of that lost world which now exists only in memory and my father's photos that give me such a tantalising glimpse into the past.

Mr Lai may have felt betrayed when my grandfather left Hong Kong. Could he have been taken with them to Australia? Probably not. Back then the White Australia policy still held sway.

So he waited patiently for the Browns to return and then, fortunately, my father did and Mr Lai had seven happy years back in the family employ.

I can't imagine what it must have been like when Dad said goodbye to him on our move back to Australia again. I think Mr Lai would have taken it pretty hard. In fact I know he did.

Because one day, several years after we returned to Australia, I found my father in his study reading a letter. I didn't know it was from Mr Lai at first, then as Dad pored over this blue aerogramme I noticed his eyes looked a little red. My father's study at our Gold Coast home was a little shrine to Hong Kong. All his office furniture had been made for him there and shipped out with our belongings. There were some Chinese artefacts and in the corner that samurai sword.

I have a crystal-clear memory of Dad on this afternoon ensconced in this domestic vessel of memories as he drank his customary glass of Scotch and read his unexpected letter.

I was intrigued that it seemed to move him. I didn't often see him like that though he was, for all his toughness, a bit of a softie and very kind-hearted.

When he left the office, taking his Scotch out onto the veranda, I stole into the office and looked at the letter left lying on his blotter.

It was from Mr Lai, telling my father in rudimentary English how everything was going well in Hong Kong and what a bright future lay ahead for the colony and how he missed the Browns and would love to work with them again. In closing he asked, in his plaintive Cantonese English tone, if my father would soon be coming back to Hong Kong.

'We are hoping so,' Mr Lai wrote. 'We love to see you back here.'

He signed off, 'With very great respect, Lai Wing-on.'

As I read his words I got a bit teary myself and thought of everything and everyone we had left behind.

CHAPTER 9

ON DEVON ROAD

It was a December Saturday in 1965 and the weather was cool. It must have been because Dad was wearing his customary cardigan and cravat, Mum one of her quilted Chinese jackets. They were sitting in our living room at Yau Yat Chuen. We had been downtown to TST for a spot of shopping and while there had gone to the record store in Mody Rd that was to become a home away from home for me in the years to come. We were on a mission to buy Christmas presents to send back to Australia and my parents had chosen an album by The Rolling Stones for my cousin Peter Reeves in Sydney.

This was the record shop where I had bought all my Beatles singles but my collection was still pretty sparse and I didn't have an LP yet. I soon would.

At the recommendation of the shopkeeper, Mum and Dad had purchased the Stones' latest album, *December's Children (and Everybody's)*. My mum's sister, Aunty Meg, had told my parents that The Rolling Stones were one of the bands Peter liked. Peter was a tad older than me and I remember on one holiday home, when the Reeves were living in West Pymble on Sydney's North Shore, Peter was in his room listening to Bob Dylan (the first time I had heard Dylan) who neither his parents nor mine could fathom. To them it wasn't even music.

The Stones weren't exactly on their wavelength either: nonetheless they purchased this album because it was the group's latest. Then off we all went to The Peninsula for morning tea. As we sat in the lobby my father pulled out the album and looked with distaste at the photo on the cover. He never quite got pop music. My mother didn't help, commenting on how scruffy and malnourished The Rolling Stones looked. Let's say they weren't exactly the right demographic to be fans and it was unusual for us to be sitting in the lobby at The Pen discussing The Rolling Stones, which is probably why the event is so memorable. I was mesmerised. The Stones looked impossibly cool.

The moody black-and-white cover image shows them huddled in an alleyway with Brian Jones, the doomed music guru, sitting in front with his hand on his chin. The others loom behind him looking like street toughs – Keith Richards with his hands in his pockets, Mick Jagger next to him pouting, Bill 'The Ghost' Wyman peering between them, and Charlie Watts off to one side brooding. It was very Beat Generation; and their producer, Andrew Loog Oldham, apparently had that in mind.

I was entranced. The problem, though, was that it wasn't my album.

When we got home with it and a batch of other presents my parents sat down in the living room to go through them all – and to listen to that record. I guess it was appropriate that it was December. To say they had misgivings about their purchase was an understatement. Being suspicious of it – judging it by its cover, you might say – they'd decided to play it to see if it was suitable. It's not really form to play someone else's record when it's a present but they did, lifting the lid on our Grundig, placing the vinyl LP on the player and sitting back on the couch to take it in. If you know the album you know it starts out hard with *She Said Yeah*, an urgent, hard-rocking number written by Sonny Bono and Roddy Jackson. This was an early Stones album and they were still doing songs written by other people. It was the last record of theirs to feature songs written by anyone other than Richards and Jagger.

The second song is *Talkin' about You*, a bluesy number by Chuck Berry. I could see by my parents' faces that, though they were only two songs in, they were already mortified. So mortified they decided not to send it to my cousin after all. I never learnt what his replacement gift was but when I heard them say they wouldn't inflict that music on anyone I hoped they would inflict it on me. So I piped up, "I'll have it."

My father looked at me as if I was mad. Mum said, "If you want it, dear, you're welcome to it." And so I acquired my first LP – on one condition. I was only allowed to play it when they were out because they found the noise so unbearable. The Rolling Stones were a long way from the music they listened to – The Kingston Trio, Bing Crosby, Andy Williams, Herb Alpert and the Tijuana Brass, my mum's favourite. She loved the tune *The Lonely Bull.*

That afternoon Mum and Dad went to the KCC and I opted to stay home and listen to the Stones. What a revelation it was. There are some killer songs on that album, it's very close to the band's rhythm-and-blues roots and I love that about it. *Look What You've Done* is a Muddy Waters song. Respect.

The beautifully lyrical ballad *As Tears Go By* is also on this album. One of the Stones' anthems is here too – *Get Off My Cloud*, a Jagger-and-Richards classic. I have only to hear the first few drumbeats and in a flash I've time-travelled back to December 1965. For me, listening to it switched a light on. I already loved The Beatles and even my parents didn't mind them, although my father once upbraided me for spending my pocket money on the monthly magazine *The Beatles Book*.

The Rolling Stones were different. Parents didn't have any time for them and I guess that was part of their allure. I loved them. My cousin Peter missed out and I was the beneficiary of that.

December's Children (and Everybody's) served as the soundtrack of our last months in Yau Yat Chuen and my last months of Year 5 at KJS. I was doing well there. In fact I was dux of Grade 4 and I still have my report card to prove it – although it's a bit weathered and worse for wear now, like some Dead Sea scroll.

I was doing well in Year 5 under the watchful eye of Miss Fung, she of the beehive hairdo and Dame Edna glasses. I say watchful because she was a hard taskmistress and took no prisoners. And because I was, for some reason, starting to misbehave a bit at school.

Two of my lifelong friends were in Grade 5A, along with me – Greg England and Timothy Budge – and a class photo still in my keeping shows us all posing on the bitumen quadrangle at KJS, Miss Fung immaculate as always in the latest suit from Lane Crawford with that sculpted hairdo making her look taller than she was.

My father's fortunes were on the rise at this time. His company was doing well and he was often away doing business in The Philippines or Thailand.

He had moved his office downtown, closer to his field office at The Pen. His new office was in Carnarvon Rd, in the same building as the French restaurant Au Trou Normand, which opened in 1964 and quickly became an iconic Kowloon eatery. Later he shifted even closer to The Pen with an office in Hankow Rd.

In Hong Kong if you were doing well you were supposed to demonstrate that with outward, even ostentatious, displays of your wealth.

In Dad's view that meant we had outgrown the flat in Wistaria Rd and needed something that befitted his growing stature in the business community. It was time for an upgrade.

So, in the summer of 1966 we moved from Yau Yat Chuen to 7 Devon Road in neighbouring Kowloon Tong, that even more gracious garden suburb.

Kowloon Tong was originally a small village and the word '*tong*' means 'pond' in Cantonese: never mind that there was no pond when we lived there. In the 1920s the Hong Kong government decided to develop the land where the village was sited, turning it into a low-density residential area based on a British model. With that in mind they named many of its streets after English counties – Devon, Cornwall, Kent and so on. This was appropriate because this neighbourhood was where English toffs lived in Kowloon, along with rich Chinese who could buy their way into the colonial world created there.

Today many of the old mansions remain, interspersed

with palatial new ones, kindergartens, schools and what are euphemistically known as 'love hotels'. Paul Theroux wrote about these in his 1997 novel *Kowloon Tong*. Theroux's take on the suburb of my salad days was a decidedly seedy one so I can assure you it was entirely respectable when we moved there in the middle of 1966. At least I think it was. Short of living at The Peak or having a house overlooking the sea at Repulse Bay, living in Kowloon Tong was *it*. Making our home there stated quite clearly that we had arrived.

Now my father had a residence that suited his mini-taipan status, which is how I think he saw himself.

7 Devon Road fitted the bill perfectly, a grand house on a big block with a high wall around most of the perimeter, which made it more of a compound really. You really couldn't see anything from the street. It would have suited Osama bin Laden down to the ground.

The house was a two-storey colonial pile that had a touch of Spanish bungalow about it with a white stucco exterior. It was solid brick and stone and that high wall surrounded it on three-and-a-half sides. There was a stretch between our place and one of the next-door homes where the fence became a low wall surmounted by a barbed-wire barrier you could see through. This meant less privacy on that part of the boundary line which was a problem because a rich Chinese family lived in that house and we didn't get on with them. They say good fences make good neighbours, and we really needed our 'Great Wall' to run along that patch too.

The wall we did have was built to keep the gracious life in and the rest of Hong Kong out. There were heavy iron gates, painted blue, at the front and a long driveway down the northern side where the driver spent hours washing and re-washing the car whether it was dirty or not.

The servants' quarters occupied the rear of the house, a small separate two-storey block where I set up my lab. I got a chemistry set shortly after we moved there and would toil over my test tubes in an upstairs room creating stink bombs and weird concoctions that Ah Moy disapproved of – probably because I was using a room in what was supposed to be the servants' domain and also, I imagine, because of the pong,

Her Spartan quarters were downstairs. Nearby was the back gate, the tradesman's entrance, which opened onto the back lane. Long lanes dissect the blocks in Kowloon Tong and run behind the houses. Here servants came and went, delivery men bought their wares, and knife sharpeners among others plied their trades, sometimes calling out as they went, their Cantonese cries rising, falling and echoing in the distance.

The front gate was for our visitors, the back gate a portal to that other Chinese world which existed for our convenience.

The front yard was expansive and crowned by several trees, including two that formed a kind of arch over the front terrace. Down one side of our new home was a large spooky playhouse, which it thrilled us to think was haunted. It had been left there by the previous inhabitants of whom we knew nothing. That strange little dwelling remained there and was largely ignored. We had the strongest feeling there was something not quite right about it.

Nearby a tall stand of bamboo separated the front from a paved backyard terrace where potted plants sat in rows forming a rather delightful Chinese garden. This area you could access via the kitchen. Our amah sat out here to eat on balmy evenings.

Downstairs our house had a large living room with a bar in one corner that would become a focus of my parents' social life. A vast dining room with barred windows looked out onto that back garden terrace. The dining table was so long it could have served as a meeting place for Churchill's war Cabinet or for dinner at Buckingham Palace. It was rarely used to its full potential because my parents didn't host many dinner parties at home. They mostly dined out.

As kids my brother and sister and I ate at one end, lonely figures in pyjamas, dwarfed by the vastness of the table, and attended by Ah Moy or, later, Ah Lun. My parents were often absent in the evenings. The cocktail party circuit was busy and there were dinners and glittering balls to distract everyone from the pressing issues of the day – the war in Vietnam, the Cold War and the Communist hordes across the border.

Walk out of our dining room and you would then come upon the grand staircase that led up to our little world of privilege. My parents' room was at the top of the stairs, overlooking the garden. It was a light and airy room that I used to steal into when they weren't home. In his bedside cabinet Dad had a cache of *Playboy* magazines – something he and Lawrence's father had in common – which I used to browse through in his absence.

The windows were barred here too, as all windows in the house were, to keep out burglars.

My sister Jane and little brother Stephen were made to share a room, which didn't seem fair really. There was, after all, a spare room at the top of the stairs that one of them could have had but it was kept free for visitors. So Jane and Steve were corralled together with a hamster called Hammy.

My room at the rear overlooking the servants' quarters and the back lane was big enough to serve as a dormitory and yet it was all – or almost all – mine. I shared it with Kitty who used to sleep curled up against my legs in a bed that was far too big for me. I had my own bathroom, and all the bathrooms at 7 Devon had bidets, which amused us. We were never quite sure how they worked but knew they were for squirting the nether regions and that made us giggle. They remained unused during our years living in that house.

I had an old Rediffusion television in my room although I was given strict instructions that I could only watch it at very limited times. It's probably safe now to reveal that I often flouted the rules with the lights off and the sound down low, watching the impossibly suave Roger Moore in *The Saint* and dreaming of my future self as an international man of mystery with perfectly Brylcreemed hair and a flashy sports car.

As I settled into that room I got a little record player which sat on the top of a low bookcase. I put pop posters up and had my stamp books within reach (I'd started my collection while living at Yau Yat Chuen). I had an air conditioner so I could stay in the room on hot summer days and pore over my stamps, listen to my burgeoning record collection and read my '*Narnia Chronicles*' or Rider Haggard adventures with our amah intermittently ferrying up sandwiches like room service at some swish hotel.

If I think of my happiest moments in life one of them would be waking in my room there one sunny morning. I opened my eyes and could see out the window pigeons lifting from a roof across the way. Down in the rear courtyard I saw Ah Moy swishing away with a broom. From the distance came the dying fall of a hawker's cry; above me was a pale blue sky. This new day, Saturday, stretched ahead of me full of promise. I looked around at my records and books, at the bugs I kept in jars on shelves and at my pop posters. God was in his heaven – all was right with the world.

If I close my eyes, even now, I am back there.

I was spoilt, I guess. Spoilt rotten, a princeling of sorts. I've never quite gotten over that. My brother and sister will probably attest to that.

To me 7 Devon Road felt more like a little palace than a house, and living there for the rest of our time in Hong Kong ruined me, there's no doubt about it.

It was a little world of privilege in a restive sea of humanity, detached from the reality beyond its confines. Resentment against us, the imperialist paper tigers that the Communists across the border railed against, would soon boil over.

All was quiet in Kowloon Tong. Too quiet. There was hardly any local traffic except for the learner drivers who came here to get away from the busy streets downtown. Little Morris Minors with L-plates on beetled round our very English streets. The red double-decker buses we sometimes used to ride came along Cornwall St. By contrast, Devon Rd was often deserted until the L-platers turned up in the afternoons. Occasionally a car would glide past, ferrying another privileged family to club or school.

Outsiders were not welcome, that was clear. The walls around our house were topped with broken glass set into concrete, making it clear to anyone who dared invade our compound that he did so at his peril.

There were parks nearby where we could play but our

garden was a world unto itself and my father, who played the occasional game of golf, set up a huge practice net in the front yard that he never used. We used to hack away at his plastic practice balls there after school.

From that front yard we had an uninterrupted view of Lion Rock, which presided over the suburb quite regally – its leonine shape clearly visible, crouched and crowning the row of hills that separated Kowloon from the rural hinterland beyond, the New Territories.

Jets heading for Kai Tak would lumber across our patch of sky, enabling us to look up at the bellies of the beasts as they lumbered towards the airport.

On summer evenings, as the light faded and Lion Rock was swallowed by darkness, tiny bats would appear, flitting across the yard, ducking and diving at the dictate of their inner radar. We would throw footballs in the air to see how efficient that guidance system truly was.

The garden was lush and constantly needed tending to. Several times a week our gardener (the *fa wong*) would arrive to toil away at controlling it.

He was one of those people who came and went silently, who straddled the divide between our world and theirs. He would arrive on a rickety bicycle that had a basket on the back in which he carried some utensils. Other tools were kept for him in a room out back in the servants' block.

Our *fa wong* was a wiry nut-brown man who wore a straw hat. He moved gracefully, like a crane, picking his way along as he perambulated around the garden clipping, weeding and watering. He also had a scythe that made him look, at times, like a cross between the Grim Reaper and a peasant farmer as he worked away, ignoring us.

On either side of a yoke that he bore across his shoulders he would sling a watering can and, tilting now this way, now that, he wandered between the rows of flowerpots out back, watering as he went. He intrigued me: there was something a little Zen and meditative about watching him at work. Years later I wrote a poem about him, *In a Kowloon Garden*, which is based on my abiding memory of him tending our garden one day during the monsoon season.

It was one of those Hong Kong days when the rain falls in torrents across the colony and we were all indoors trying to amuse ourselves. On this day I sat in the dining room, at the end of that vast dining table, working on some school project and looking up now and then to gaze on the unrelenting deluge outside. At one stage I took a break from my labours and walked to the back of the dining room to look out at the back courtyard and, as I did, the rain started to pelt down heavier than ever.

It had caused a kind of mist to form that shrouded the terrace and gave it the look of a scene from a Chinese scroll, some mountain garden in the clouds, a scene glimpsed and recorded in poetry by some sage-cum-bard. I paused, enjoying the scene, and was amazed to see the *fa wong* out there in the weather. He was wearing a shiny raincoat and his customary straw hat which now had a plastic covering on it.

Despite the fact that it was pouring with rain, he was watering the plants in his time-honoured way, moving along the rows slowly and diligently. It made no sense, of course, but he had a job to do and was doing it. All this while our

Kowloon garden continued being watered from two sources simultaneously: one the annual drenching monsoon, the other – equally predictable, equally reliable – a wistful figure, human nature in a straw hat overflowing with water.

CHAPTER 10

THE KOWLOON KID

The night of the attempted burglary of our house in Kowloon Tong stands as symbolic proof that all was not as well as it seemed in Hong Kong in the spring of 1966. The burglary occurred when our family was well and truly settled in at 7 Devon Road.

Late at night there was a scream – my mother sounding like an extra in a horror movie – and we all got out of bed to see what was wrong. Ah Moy had come running up the staircase and by then Mum was at the bedroom door having what she would have called a conniption.

My father, dozing with the moonlight streaming into the bedroom, had half woken to see a hand coming through the window. An arm with a hand, actually. Looking back, I imagine it as a scene from one of those B-grade horror movies where dismembered limbs come to life and go on rampages with evil intent. This arm was reaching in through the barred window that overlooked my father's sturdy rosewood bedside table. On the table was his watch, a gold Rolex Oyster Perpetual Day Date. I know that sounds like an advertisement so before you jump to the conclusion that this is some kind of product placement I should point out that I remember the brand and the model so well because I coveted that watch. For me it was a kind of touchstone, an object that reeked of Sixties style. I think of it nostalgically, not materialistically.

My father would keep it his whole life. He was wearing it when he died. In my grief then, I wasn't thinking much about the watch. Years later, my thoughts turned to it again and I wondered about its fate. Did my mother sell it? I was never sure. But it seems to have just disappeared, kind of like the Ark of the Covenant. There is a vintage watch shop in historic old Brisbane Arcade where I often stop and look longingly at the gold Rolexes in the window.

Of course that one was worth a bit of money and the burglar who had the audacity to breach our perimeter must have thought he had hit pay dirt when on looking through the open window he saw it sitting there, glinting in the moonlight. My father always took it off to sleep. The window was open because it was presumed there was no need to close a barred window. Against this burglar, there was. His arm was just long enough to reach in and grab the Rolex. Dad later told the story of how he had awoken and seen that paw reach for the watch, inching forward. He said he had been dozy at first and thought it must have been a dream. Considering how soundly he slept I'm surprised my father didn't just snore his way through the whole episode. Mum usually slept fitfully and even later in life when staying with her you would hear her wake in fright in the night and call out. Ignore her and she would soon go back to sleep.

That night she obviously sensed something amiss and, half

conscious, sat up, saw the hand through the bars reaching for my father's watch, and screamed. As she did so the hand, with burglar attached, latched onto the prize. Dad instantly sat up and gave that arm an almighty karate chop, possibly with sound effects. I imagine he may have sworn in Cantonese at the same moment. He could curse like a local.

The hand dropped the watch and quickly withdrew. The person attached to it must then have jumped from the ledge onto the front terrace. My father looked out the window to see this figure tearing across the yard like a cut cat.

All this had happened not long before we arrived at my parents' bedroom door. It was rather exciting really. The police were called, a European officer attended and blood was found in the jagged glass atop the front wall where the burglar had obviously cut himself on the way in or out, perhaps even both.

Dad had connections in the Hong Kong police force and he knew the officer who turned up. The police force was run mostly by British officers and was very efficient, even if it was rotten to the core. Dad had a secretary in Hong Kong – an Englishwoman, Mavis Cunningham – whose husband, a bear of a man yet known to us as 'Moose', was caught up in a big corruption scandal, jailed in the colony and later deported home. It was, so people would quip, the best police force that money could buy and that sort of activity didn't help the reputation of the British-run administration amid rumblings about colonial rule.

We were beginning to hear such rumblings and the visible expression of discontent came in the form of posters that local Communist cadres were starting to plaster around Kowloon – posters showing Western capitalists as figures of fun, even sometimes, as dogs – imperialist running dogs, in the Maoist cant of the day. We were also 'paper tigers', a literal translation of the Chinese phrase *zhilaohu*, denoting something or someone that seems threatening but is actually ineffectual and unable to withstand challenge.

In 1966, around the time of the unsuccessful burglary on our stately colonial pile, those early rumblings of discontent had boiled to the surface. I have always seen that botched robbery as the starting point of the troubles to come.

Deep inside our colonial bubble it escaped our notice that all was not well for those without. As refugees poured across the border, living conditions for many Chinese in Hong Kong deteriorated and thousands lived in squalid squatters' villages as the government struggled to catch up and build public housing for them.

Mao's disastrous Great Leap Forward between 1958 and 1961 had accelerated the refugee flow, sending hundreds of thousands south.

The police and British Army built a barbed-wire fence along the frontier and still they came, crawling under it or evading it by swimming or arriving by boat along Hong Kong's ragged coastline.

In April '66 the Star ferry fares, which have always been ludicrously cheap, were increased, sparking protests and eventually riots at the terminals on either side of the harbour. One protestor was killed and many were jailed.

The following month the Cultural Revolution was launched across the border. As kids, we were blissfully unaware of the winds and crosswinds of history swirling all about us but, being the oldest, I did pick up bits and pieces and would sometimes hear my parents and their friends discussing the Communist menace.

Things settled down for a while after that although the following year they would re-erupt in far more ominous and deadly fashion.

Looking back now, I'm amazed at how free I was to roam the streets. There was no such thing as helicopter parenting back in the day. From the age of nine I travelled by myself to and from TST and started spending a lot of time at the home of one of my best friends, Greg England, who lived downtown.

The Englands occupied the penthouse of a building called Telephone House on the corner of Cameron and Nathan Roads. Don't go looking for that building now though because, like most of historical Hong Kong, it was demolished long ago and replaced, appropriately enough, by a bank.

Telephone House was the sort of gracious old apartment building you might find in New York. Its ground floor and basement were given over to a department store called Whiteaway's; up top, the spacious and airy England residence was surrounded by the usual barred windows.

It became my base camp over the long summer break of 1966 and for the next couple of years.

Despite their surname the Englands were ethnic exotics. Their background was Chinese, Portuguese and English, with Greg's parents, Harold and Lorraine, both born in Shanghai. His dad had been interned by the Japanese and his parents fled the Communists to reach Hong Kong. That Shanghai background had a kind of mystique to it, then as now. It was where old Cathay met the West. In its heyday it had been the home of Chinese cinema and The Bund was one of the world's most famous waterfronts. Hong Kong restaurants and bars often try to replicate Shanghai style and the Hong Kong tycoon David Tang even created a retail brand, Shanghai Tang – emblematic of that great city's glory days.

Greg's parents being from Shanghai – where my grandfather's Chinese odyssey had begun – made a deep impression on me.

His dad, Harold, was in the property business and their apartment was stunning. If you had one in that location now it would be worth millions.

I used to catch a London-style double-decker bus from Kowloon Tong and hop off in Nathan Rd near Greg's place in bustling downtown Tsim Sha Tsui. Vibrant now, TST was more exotic in the mid-Sixties and – despite the riots and patches of seediness – mostly safe. It was our playground, our backyard.

There were always plenty of police around, including military police, due to the increasing numbers of servicemen on rest-and-recreation leave from the Vietnam War. Red Peril paranoia was fuelled by that war as well as by the restiveness across the border.

Greg and I would roam through TST, often passing groups of soldiers and sailors heading for some of the girlie bars that had sprung up in the streets nearby.

Girls would stand outside touting for business and occasionally call out to us as we wandered past. "Hey Johnny," one bargirl said to me one day. "You like drink? Maybe girl?" I mean, did I not look 10 years old?

We lived with the mystery of exactly what went on behind the beaded curtains that hung across the doorways to some of these bars, which operated around the clock to – if you'll pardon the phrase – service the servicemen.

Greg and I would pass these bars on our way to a street market where we used to buy eggs. This market was in a narrow lane that ran between two parallel roads, Cameron and Granville. The market sold fresh produce and fish for eating, as well as those 100-year-old eggs that made us gag just to look at and pet goldfish in plastic bags filled with water. The stuff that Chinese people ate was beyond my comprehension and the idea that anyone could eat a dog was simply shocking to us.

We would buy rotten eggs here because they were cheaper and smellier. Perfect for throwing. I still can't figure out what else people would have wanted to do with them.

Above Greg's apartment was a flat rooftop area. Rising above it was a wonderful old clock tower with a four-sided face in the middle of it. Inside the tower were the servants' quarters where the Englands' amahs lived.

When nobody was around we would go up onto the roof with our arsenal of market eggs and, strategically placed like some crazy snipers, lob them down onto busy Nathan Rd far below. Shocking vandalism, I know, but we really thought it was great fun. Even now when I walk along that stretch of Nathan Rd I instinctively look up half expecting to see eggs raining down. All I see is the bank that towers above the spot where Telephone House once stood.

Our principal targets were the double-decker buses running up and down Nathan Rd, the stretch of downtown Kowloon they call the Golden Mile. When an egg hit the roof of one of those buses there was an almighty bang which gave us a certain satisfaction. After hurling these projectiles we would hide out in the clock tower until we reckoned it was safe enough to come out again.

Greg's parents were usually out so no one knew our secret. Unless the amahs suspected us?

The building that abutted Greg's on the south was Majestic House which included the Majestic Guest House. Nice name for a knocking shop, we thought, because we suspected that it was just another house of ill repute and it certainly wasn't very majestic.

We would spend hours waiting by the window, peering through the bars trying to catch a glimpse of scantily clad Chinese women who, wisely, pulled the curtains closed most of the time. Now and then we would see one glide past the window like a silhouette on a Chinese screen.

Another way we passed the time that long summer of 1966 was making hoax phone calls to numbers chosen at random out of the phone book.

When someone answered I would say: "Hello, my name is Melwani, you want to buy Indian carpet?" I got that line from a bloke who had a shop in a nearby arcade, a spivvy Indian with a quiff and pointy shoes who reeked of some exotic scent.

Some days would be spent at the YMCA or the 'Y' on Salisbury Rd, one of the centres of our little colonial world. The Y had, and still has, a prime position on the Kowloon waterfront just across the road from The Peninsula, that other hub of social life. The Y retains its function to this day, now also boasting a high-rise hotel, The Salisbury. The original low colonial building was long ago knocked down and, like much of Hong Kong's past, it exists only in old photos or our memories. Most Europeans who spent part of their childhoods in Hong Kong back in the Sixties will have spent time at the Y.

We took afternoon tea there a couple of years ago with my former school chum David McKirdy who still lives in Hong Kong and has never actually left. His family came out from Scotland and his father was in shipping. David is a well-known Hong Kong poet with a wonderful sideline: he travels the world servicing and repairing vintage and classic cars and is a consultant to The Peninsula group on these matters, among others. He lives in rustic Hoi Ha Village in Sai Kung Country Park.

We hooked up again some years ago through a photo posted on Facebook of three boys in a hurdles race at King George V School sometime in the late Sixties. One is me, one my pal Mark Reeve and the third was David McKirdy who hadn't known that I was the third person in the photo until I pointed it out. David and I have bonded over our shared avocation, poetry. As we took tea at the Y we recalled the glory days there and its infamous swimming pool.

The water in that pool was white and we reckoned it had to be the most chlorinated pool on the planet: it was like swimming in disinfectant. You couldn't open your eyes underwater and when you floated in it your lower limbs weren't visible. After a swim there you stank of chlorine for days. It was said that the club had been so unsure about the sanitariness of patrons – Chinese, Europeans and others – that it decided to create a chemical environment capable of killing anything. Possibly even those who swam in it.

As well as swimming there – which we were forced to do at times – we spent our time playing ping pong. Gymnastics classes and some cultural activities were also available. This was before the age of political correctness and we once did a Black and White Minstrel Show. I still know all the words to *By the Light of the Silvery Moon* and we also sang *Michael Row the Boat Ashore* and *Swing Low, Sweet Chariot*, among other tunes. We used make-up to blacken our faces.

On our days of roaming round TST Greg England and I would often stop off at the Y café for lunch – hot dogs served by ancient diffident waiters in starched white jackets. Starched and white as the jackets were, they usually featured stains that obviously never quite came out. We would browse in the little bookstore there afterwards (there is still one there on Salisbury Rd to this day) where I bought my first Biggles book.

For me, places and times in Hong Kong are marked by the release of important pop records and I always identify the Englands' apartment with The Beatles' *Revolver* album which came out that summer of 1966. I was already a Beatles tragic and for me *Revolver* was nothing short of a spiritual experience. I bought it, and all my records, from that little shop in Mody Rd very close to Greg England's pad.

The Chinese guy who ran it was very pop-savvy, always playing music, spinning discs down the back of the store. One day when we went in he was playing some Motown stuff for some black American servicemen who were jiving along to it. The experience was like watching a movie. They were in mufti, and not just ordinary mufti – these guys, looking cool in tight trousers and colourful satin shirts, were grooving to the music much to the delight of the storekeeper who looked anything but cool in his black trousers and white shirt. He dressed like an office clerk and had an unfortunate overbite.

I bought *Revolver* from him as soon as it came out and took the LP back to Greg's place to play it. I can still recall those first few moments listening to the beginning of the opening song, George Harrison's *Taxman,* a Sixties protest song with a difference.

If their previous album, *Rubber Soul,* had been life-changing for me, *Revolver* was a new world altogether. It was the album that ushered in the Fab Four's psychedelic phase with sitar and enigmatic songs such as John Lennon's *Tomorrow Never Knows* with Beat poetry lyrics and what sound like weird seagull sound effects; and Harrison's *Love You To* which introduced us all to classical Indian sitar music.

If you're a Beatles fan like me you will have had your favourite Beatle. Mine was always John. It wasn't until I was older, though, that I realised I shared a birthday with him, October 9. I take that to be significant.

That day we played *Revolver* over and over and over again in the Englands' eyrie, high above the streets of Kowloon.

Greg was handy to hang out with because he spoke Cantonese. It was his first language actually, and as a young boy he had learnt it from an illiterate amah by the name of Ah Soh who was, so he tells me, raised aboard a sampan in Macau.

My Cantonese was rudimentary, to say the least, and still is. I can order coffee or tea and direct a taxi where to go and, importantly, I can swear but that's about it. As kids we learnt the common Cantonese curses first and foremost. Some are quite inappropriate because they involve one's mother while others cast aspersions on family and ancestry.

Greg's Cantonese is still pretty good and I know that because we had lunch together just over a year ago in Brighton, England, where he now lives with his wife, Jackie, although technically they are just along the coast in Hove. We had yum cha, of course, and I left the ordering to him with his superior Cantonese. We have kept in touch ever since those early days together in Kowloon.

I'm not sure if he remembers this but one day we got involved in a rickshaw race with some American servicemen. Rickshaws were still a common form of transport in the Sixties. In fact one of the earliest photos I have from my boyhood days shows me and my little brother Stephen in a rickshaw drawn by a bloke who was almost a caricature – a wiry dark-skinned Chinese man with buck teeth who my father paid to drag us up and down Middle Rd (the road that runs behind The Peninsula) as a sort of rite of passage.

In the Sixties they had only just stopped using sedan chairs. I have a friend who recalls that his mother used to be ferried up The Peak in a sedan chair, the ultimate colonial indulgence. Pity the poor coolies who did the hauling.

Rickshaws may have been a little more humane than sedan chairs: still, they were a form of transport that came close to slave labour at times. At the same time it was a regular job in Hong Kong back in the day.

As kids we used them occasionally. My father never travelled in them, though, because he was quite portly and had a certain regard for rickshaw drivers.

One day Greg England and I had been across to Hong Kong side on the Star ferry. I can't recall what we were doing over there: we were probably up to no good.

When we arrived back at the Kowloon-side Star ferry terminal it was raining, that Hong Kong rain which caused landslides and back then wreaked havoc with squatters.

Normally we would walk from the Star ferry to Greg's place. With the rain pouring down we commandeered a rickshaw. The drivers used to line up near the terminal sitting in front of their distinctive red conveyances with green canopies that could be pulled up in inclement weather. I guess you could say those rickshaws were convertibles.

So our driver pulled up the canopy and took off, trotting along Salisbury Rd in the incessant downpour. First we passed the YMCA, then The Peninsula, and then turned left into Nathan Rd, the Golden Mile stretching ahead of us. As he gathered pace another couple of rickshaws pulled alongside us. They were laden with US Navy men in their white sailor uniforms.

It soon became apparent that they were drunk. They were shouting a lot and apparently wanted a race, pretending to whip the rickshaw boys who didn't look all that impressed. They were forced to go faster and, as they did, our guy kept up with them.

So down Nathan Rd we went, the sailors bellowing at the rickshaw-pullers to go faster as we passed Chungking Mansions and headed for the corner of Cameron Rd. Our competitors seemed disappointed when we pulled over and got out: still, they continued down Cameron Rd and I'm sure that before too long they would have been happily ensconced in some girlie bar where they could live out their Suzie Wong fantasies.

Returning to Hong Kong as an adult I have occasionally tried to conjure the past by riding in rickshaws, despite this being a politically incorrect mode of travel. I have always felt sorry for the drivers lined up in dwindling numbers outside the Star ferry Hong Kong-side terminal. By the early 1970s locals had ceased to use the rickshaw as a regular mode of transport, relegating it to the exclusive status of tourist attraction. Around 1975 the last rickshaw licence was issued. By then there were only around 100 left, and fewer and fewer 'rickshaw boys', as they were known regardless of age.

As the years went by there was less and less work for them, and most were hired by tourists just for photo opportunities.

This I have done time and again, much to my wife's embarrassment. I have always felt quite comfy sitting in a rickshaw, and have argued that at least I was helping the rickshaw boys earn a living even if I looked like a goose posing in a painted buggy like some second-rate potentate.

In 21st-century Hong Kong they disappeared altogether from the scene.

Some years ago when there were just a few left I had my last ride in one. We had caught a Star ferry over to Hong Kong side. Of course you don't have to cross by ferry with the MTR being a more efficient way but to me it's a ritual and one of the world's great ferry rides, albeit a short one. And the fares are still crazy cheap. The terminals haven't been tarted up and still look basically the way they did when I was a kid. The ritual, too, is the same – all wait behind the gate until the bells ring and then you take part in a collective stampede down the walkway and across the wooden gangway to board.

One of the first things I learnt in Cantonese was how to say "Star ferry" (*tin sing maa tau*), which is handy when you get into a taxi and want to go there.

And so, after crossing the harbour, Sandra and I went to walk past the last few rickshaw boys, all seemingly ancient men who sat smoking, resigned to their own extinction. I stopped in front of one and he looked up and smiled at me on realising he had a potential fare. I simply couldn't say no.

He beckoned for me to get in and I asked Sandra to get ready to take a photo. He insisted on going down the concourse then onto the road that runs alongside Admiralty. Sandra, embarrassed, followed as the poor bloke dragged me along.

Like some remnant of the Raj I posed for my photo and Sandra begged me to get out because a smallish crowd had gathered, and they were taking their own photos of this scene from the sepia past, of an imperialist-running-dog colonial master being pulled in a cart by a coolie.

It was then that my rickshaw boy – I can only assume he wanted to give me my money's worth – started moving forward and pointing ahead. He seemed hellbent on taking me for a proper ride.

Sandra looked worried. I turned around, looked at her and called out, "I'll be back in a minute."

We were on a quiet stretch of road where taxis pull in to drop people and he went along there at a snail's pace at first: then, gaining momentum, he veered out into a lane of traffic. I think he had a rush of blood to the head, his glory days flooding back, and so we were off, him trotting proudly along as cars sounded their horns and tore past us, me in the back, terrified. Bemused tourists gawked from the sidewalk and some were even waving. They seemed delighted that old Hong Kong had come to life in front of their very eyes.

Suddenly the driver wilted. He turned around and headed back to the pick-up point and when he delivered me to my waiting wife I paid him, adding a generous tip for which he seemed most grateful and said, "*Doh jeh, doh jeh.*"

"Well, that was embarrassing," was all she said.

Now the rickshaw men and their shiny steeds have all gone. If you want to see one of those distinctive red gigs in today's SAR (since 1997 Hong Kong's status in China is that of 'Semi-Autonomous Region'), you need to visit the excellent Hong Museum of History in Tsim Sha Tsui East.

I keep some in my own museum – my memory – where they are perfectly preserved and largely impervious to the ravages of time.

CHAPTER 11

REMEMBER THE SIDETRACKS

Because I write a weekly column about my life, every so often I mention my time in Hong Kong. OK, I mention it *more* than every so often. I confess it: I'm a Hong Kong bore in the same way that John Howard is a cricket tragic. My column, which appears in the lifestyle magazine *Brisbane News*, is pretty personal and, as I have come to understand, well read. I can gauge that by the number of people I meet in the supermarket, and elsewhere, who happen to know that I have a tartan dressing gown. See, I have written about that too. I have written more about Hong Kong than I have about my dressing gown, though, which you'll be relieved to hear. And I do get correspondence related to all this. As they say in the classics, keep those cards and letters coming in, folks.

A few years ago I got contacted about one of my Hong Kong columns.

It came in the form of a query. "Phil, were you in a band in Hong Kong in the Sixties?" The query came from a woman called Judy Seaton. The name didn't ring a bell.

Her query made me smile for a moment. I answered,

somewhat tentatively: "Yes, fleetingly, but it was just kids. We were called The Sidetracks."

"Yes, that's the one I'm thinking of," she replied.

And this is where it got so weird and serendipitous that I still get a little tingle down my spine when I think about it. She remembered The Sidetracks?

We had done an end-of-school-year concert (I guess you could call it a gig) at Kowloon Junior School in 1967. Judy Seaton, who now lives in Brisbane's leafy west, knew about the gig because she was there. Turns out she was one of the go-go dancers that day – one of two. There was Judy, who was then Judith Chalmers. At the time she happened to be the girlfriend of my pal Mark Reeve who was sexually precocious, to put it mildly.

The other girl was Debbie Taylor. Judith was Scottish and Debbie English. When Judy contacted me they both lived in southeast Queensland. Judy was in the *Brisbane News* readership catchment area, which is how she came to read my column and twig that I might have been the same Phillip Brown (I was usually Phillip in those days rather than Phil) who was the quasi-charismatic co-lead singer of a very short-lived Hong Kong pop music phenomenon. The Sidetracks blazed like a shooting star, then sank like a stone.

Judy was in Brisbane, Debbie on the Gold Coast, so it was agreed we should meet for coffee.

Judy told me her mum had taken a photo of the gig with both girls dancing out front below the stage in matching mini-skirts and white go-go boots, with us in the background. This meant that there was a photo extant of The Sidetracks, which is kind of like finding out that someone has a snapshot of a yeti. Judy promised to get her mother, back in Edinburgh, to rifle through her photo box in an effort to dig it up. I'm still waiting for that.

The Sidetracks was a fleeting experience. Any shorter and I'd have missed it altogether. It was a pop group (it was pop, not rock back then) consisting of four ten-year-old Grade 6 kids at KJS.

We appeared just the once, like Brigadoon, that mysterious Scottish village in the Lerner-and-Lowe musical, which appears out of the mist for only one day in every 100 years and then is gone.

The Sidetracks' nano-moment in the limelight was on a wonky wooden stage at the fag end of the school year. The dawn of the Summer of Love wasn't far off. Meanwhile we had our own in that tiny hall, in that little school, in the middle of Kowloon in the 1960s.

Hong Kong was pop-mad at the time. It was the Oriental counterpart of Swinging London. British pop music and fashion had been embraced by Westerners and local Chinese alike. It was all the rage, a frenzy turbocharged by the hordes of visiting servicemen and fed by the BBC, local pop radio stations and a burgeoning local band scene. Teddy Robin and the Playboys, fronted by an unlikely guy with a hunchback (who went on to become an actor and film director), was the hot Hong Kong band of the day and they would go on to be the stars of *Soundbeat '67*, Hong Kong's version of Britain's *Top of the Pops* or Australia's *Countdown*. *Soundbeat '67* aired on the colony's first television channel, RTV.

British pop magazines also fuelled the music mania. I was a devotee of *Fabulous 208* (*Fab 208* as it was better known).

I'd devoured it religiously since its first issue appeared in 1964. The doors of my bedroom cupboard in Kowloon Tong were plastered with photos of pop stars cut out of the mag. I never cut up my copies of *The Beatles Book* though. They were sacred and stored in a little pile in my bookcase. Pictures of The Beatles and other pop stars from *Fab 208* and other sources were sticky-taped to the cupboard door.

My father used to get quite annoyed that most of my pocket money went on pop records and magazines. Any left over was spent on stamps and books. None of this resonated with him because he wasn't a reader and seemed to resent my being such a bookworm. As I've already pointed out, the man didn't read books. When he was sick in bed in Hong Kong my mother used to buy him those *Commando* comic books that were so popular at the time. He would read them or construction plans and specifications. I don't think he ever read a serious novel thought I wonder if he might have actually glanced through some of those sexy Carter Brown crime stories that were bestsellers in the Sixties. They were by an English-born Australian writer whose real name was Alan Geoffrey Yates. I remember finding one on his bedside table during one of those secret forays into my parents' bedroom. The Carter Brown novel featured a semi-naked woman on the cover. That memory has just flashed into my mind and now I wonder if I may have underestimated my father? Pulp fiction is still fiction, after all.

But he didn't share my interests and wasn't enthusiastic about my pastimes. Why, he wondered, would I want to spend so much time in my room reading, listening to music or rearranging my stamp albums?

Around the time I was in The Sidetracks I was also getting quite serious and nerdy about stamp collecting. I frequented a philately outlet at the Ocean Terminal near the Star ferry quay Kowloon-side. That shopping mall was new and flashy then and is still there, tarted up of course. The Ocean Terminal is conjoined with that vast enclave of shopping arcades called Harbour City and now, besides ferry terminals, it incorporates hotels as well as cruise-ship berths. The arcades there are somewhat labyrinthine and I usually get lost. Back in the day I bought all my stamps at Ocean Terminal and every year I keenly awaited and obsessively collected the special first-day cover issued for Chinese New Year. I may still have a collection of them somewhere in a camphorwood box.

I started specialising too and chose fairly obscure countries to focus on: Bhutan and Papua New Guinea (believe it or not, PNG – then an Australian trust territory – seems obscure when you're in Hong Kong). Stamps from there were very exotic and I had some gorgeous sets featuring colourful birds of paradise. I would hole up in my room poring over my albums and my Stanley Gibbons catalogue, the philatelists' bible (it was actually thicker than the Bible).

If I wasn't attending to my stamps or reading I was listening to records on my portable record player.

I had a hankering to be a pop star, no doubt about it. I had a small acoustic guitar that I was attempting to teach myself to play, without much success. Also in my bedroom were a set of bongos and a small snare drum my parents had bought me.

I was pretty engrossed with all this and at home tended to live in my own little world a lot of the time, often ignoring what my brother and sister were up to. We were a close family in many ways but being the eldest I was always slightly detached.

Much of the time I was in my room dreaming of my future life as a pop star. As part of that, I wanted to look like one of The Beatles. This ambition was thwarted by my father who was of the opinion that long hair was for girls. So he wouldn't let me grow mine. I did everything in my power to try to convince my mother to postpone our haircuts (my little brother and I usually went together) so that I could develop a mop top. My earlier style, Brylcreem with a quiff, was by now so last-decade.

Our barber in The Peninsula arcade wasn't a butcher like those early snippers we went to and I like to think he had some sympathy for my position. If he seemed to be taking too much off I would whisper to him to stop cutting. He had magazines in his shop featuring pictures of pop stars so his clientele could request a certain style and he was happy to oblige but my father would not be happy if I turned up home from the barber-shop as hirsute as I was before the visit. Besides, he would see the result sooner rather than later since our haircuts were usually followed by a pit stop in The Peninsula lobby.

Desperate to acquire the Beatle look I would even brush my short hair down on all sides – if that's all I had left. I had to content myself with that.

My pop obsession was shared by some of my school chums, including the pop music guru of Grade 6 at KJS, a musical Svengali by the name of Chris Nelson. Being tall, blond and American, he had the trifecta – and his parents did let him grow his hair a bit. So he actually looked like a pop star while I was busy trying to.

It must have been around autumn 1966 when he formed The Sidetracks and somehow I managed to talk my way into the line-up.

We four were fab enough: me and three Americans – Chris; our drummer, Scott Gepford; and Robert Hafner, who was co-lead singer with me. Chris was lead guitarist and the band's music brain, a kind of cross between Brian Jones and Mike Nesmith. Musically, though, we were pretty thin. All we had was an acoustic guitar played by Chris (I couldn't yet play mine well enough for the band), a drum, cymbals, some maracas and a tambourine which Robert Hafner and I took turns with. Chris and Scott were both quite tall, Robert about my height, and we formed a duo, like Peter and Gordon.

Pop music was our shared obsession and we rehearsed whenever we could – at Scott's place, I think, because that's where the drum kit was located.

In class 6R we had a teacher called Mrs Bramwell, a little genial dumpling of a woman who was very English – she would have made a good Miss Marple – and very charming. And inspiring. I did very well in her class despite being somewhat distracted by my music and the band.

Music pervaded all our waking thoughts. I remember one day in Mrs Bramwell's class we were playing charades and when it was Chris Nelson's turn to do his mime he combed his blond thatch down over his eyes, stood up in front of the class and acted out his subject. It was an album title. Chris pointed madly at his shirt and the class was mystified until I picked up on it. He was pointing at the spaces between the buttons on the front of his shirt, which is how I twigged. "*Between the Buttons*," I shouted out. It was a cracking album by The

Rolling Stones that came out in January 1967. That was a few months before our big gig – our one and only gig.

How we came to have one at all I'm unsure of although Mrs Versloot, the headmistress, was pretty groovy and totally up with Sixties music as well as fashion. Somehow or other she had got wind of the fact that certain of her senior boys had formed a pop group and with that we were engaged to do a concert in front of the whole school to wind up the school year.

It was exciting and a little daunting. We would have to rehearse and appear on stage, the same stage that had been the cause of my ejection from the school choir. We had been performing a recital of some sort, singing English folk songs. We were in tiers (that's right, not tears), some kids sitting on the floor in front, others kneeling behind them and a row of us standing on a bench at the back, raised above the others. I was on the end of the row in the middle of the traditional English song *Oh No, John* when someone pushed me off just as we got to the chorus. I fell onto the stage in mid-performance and lay there, spreadeagled on the wooden boards for a few seconds before I got up, dusted myself off, climbed back up to my allotted perch and continued. I thought this was pretty good showmanship but when the show was over I was sacked from the choir. Which was fine really because it gave me latitude to concentrate on my career as a pop star.

Once we had been engaged to play the gig we had some work to do getting together a programme of songs. Chris Nelson, the maestro, was in charge of that. He was a guy whose conversation was punctuated by the expression "Hey, man". We thought American accents were cool. It was quite infectious really, being in a band with three Americans. It made me want to speak American too, like my dad. I remember my father often coming home with an American twang if he'd been drinking with Yanks, which he sometimes did. He seemed to enjoy their company and after an hour or two with them would adopt their accent and turn up at home still talking like that, possibly the worse for wear. One day he brought an American sailor (in uniform) home after meeting him in Conder's Bar, one of his favourite Kowloon watering holes, and I think my father's American accent was actually thicker than the Yank's.

In The Sidetracks I was surrounded by these American accents, which was strange considering the fact that we were in a British colony in the middle of a British pop 'invasion'. Notwithstanding that, our dress code for the band would be unambiguously British. For our concert we decided to wear a uniform, as The Beatles did after Brian Epstein became their manager. Not suits, mind you, but certainly Beatle boots. We all had a pair. We would also wear tight blue jeans with blue turtleneck sweaters and brush our hair down so that we resembled the Fab Four or some other band straight out of Merseyside.

Though some of the set list for our gig is lost in the mists of time I still recall the highlights. *Black Is Black* by Los Bravos, which had been released the previous August and had done well in the charts, was one of the numbers we played that day. Los Bravos lead singer Mike Kogel's vocals were so reminiscent of Gene Pitney's that some people thought it was Pitney singing. The song was receiving a lot of radio play and Chris Nelson liked it so we rehearsed it as one of our signature pieces. Robert Hafner and I sang it on stage using one of those little megaphones they used for sports day to project our voices. Attached to the megaphone – which sat at the front of the stage – was a microphone, which we shared.

As we sang, Judy and Debbie pranced around in front of the stage while the audience sat there rapt. At least I assume they were rapt. My sister was among the assembled throng and she recalls feeling rather proud of her pop-star older brother. Debbie and Judy wore those knee-high white go-go boots that were all the rage at the time and their mini-skirts.

The only other song I recall from that gig was the hero piece, Chris Nelson's big starry number … American Barry McGuire's 1965 protest song *Eve of Destruction*, which sounds an odd choice for a group of ten-year-olds. But Chris was way ahead of us all and this was his anthem, so it just had to be sung.

It was, it must be said, a tad apocalyptic for a primary school audience. I still remember seeing a look of concern on one teacher's face as we sang of adult fears, denouncing hate, hypocrisy, bloodletting – and, what must have horrified every adult in the room because of its 'security implications', a starkly disturbing vision of the Eastern world exploding.

In retrospect it was the perfect song for that place and time. I mean here we were in a little colonial enclave at the tip of Communist China in the middle of the Cold War with the conflict in Vietnam gathering pace and the murderous Cultural Revolution beginning just across the border.

I couldn't imagine a more fitting number, really. *Eve of Destruction* was perfectly suited for singing in Hong Kong in 1967 (one line even references 'Red China').

OK, the assembled throng, Grades 1-6 at KJS, may not

have been the right audience for it yet they seemed happy enough clapping along as Judy and Debbie clumped away in their go-go boots.

I remember standing there on that stage, nervous as hell, singing my heart out. My dream of pop stardom was realised, for one fleeting moment, long ago and far away.

I'm not sure why the band fizzled out after that. There was no dramatic break-up, or none that I can recall. We just dispersed and soon we would all be moving up to King George V School next door. My pop obsession would only grow in the ensuing year. Alas, The Sidetracks wouldn't be part of it. Mine may have been the shortest pop career in history.

And it all came back to me when Judy Seaton contacted me out of the blue. At the time of writing she is still hunting for that photo of the gig, of her and Debbie doing their thing out front while we banged and wailed away on that little stage.

I don't know if I really need the photo, though. If I close my eyes now I can see it all quite clearly. There's Chris Nelson, eyes half closed, flicking his fringe out of his eyes as he sings *Eve of Destruction* while I bang the tambourine and chime in with Robert Hafner, our voices blaring out through that tinny little megaphone. That there was my 15 minutes of fame. Thank you, Andy Warhol.

CHAPTER 12

MAN WITH THE GOLDEN SMILE

Lee's smile always lit up a room. Not because he had a sunny disposition, though he did seem to be a reasonably agreeable chap: rather because he had a mouth full of gold teeth that glinted in whatever light was available.

'Little Lee' wasn't really so small. He was of a normal build, a middle-aged Chinese man who wore cheap suits and white shirts but never a tie. He had a salt-and-pepper crew cut with a flat top. It was such a fine, grey, bristly thatch I reckon you could have filed your nails on it. I'm assuming he was called Little Lee because somewhere on my father's staff there was another, bigger Lee. Actually there were a few Lees, so the potential for confusion was undeniable.

I first came across Little Lee while visiting my father's building sites and he had visited us at home in Kowloon Tong on Chinese New Year 1966. Come Chinese New Year 1967, which fell on February 9 in accordance with the Chinese astrological calendar, Little Lee failed to turn up at our house for the usual festivities.

It was the Year of the Sheep, or Ram, or Goat, depending

on who you talk to. We celebrated two New Years, the Western one first. It was marked by those big family days at the Kowloon Cricket Club. A few weeks afterwards – it depended on the lunar cycle – we would get Chinese New Year with all its customary colour, fireworks displays and feasting.

On Chinese New Year's Day some of my father's employees would visit our house bearing gifts and chanting "*Gung hei fat choi, gung hei fat choi*" ("Wishing you good fortune and happiness"). There was no gold, frankincense or myrrh … instead they came laden with Chinese goodies including boxes of *wah mui* (dried plums), dried beef and other sometimes questionable comestibles. Boxes of cigars and bottles of cognac were also proffered and Dad would dole out bonuses in red packets (*lai see*) as is customary at that time of year.

Around Chinese New Year, when Hong Kong is cooler than some people expect it to be, my father's senior staff came to pay homage to their boss and on this day in 1967 one of them came down the driveway carrying two big brown paper bags that sparked our curiosity. As he approached we realised that something was moving inside these bags and both were beginning to make clucking sounds.

They were presented to my father and my mother. Somewhat perplexed, Mum looked down into them. She obviously wasn't thrilled with what she saw there but, trying to sound enthusiastic, she said, "Oh look … chickens!" Dad made a slight bow, uttered, "*Doh jeh, doh jeh*" and called our new amah, Ah Lun, to take care of the fowls as he greeted the visitors and accepted their gifts.

Ah Lun replaced Ah Moy, who had, like Little Lee, disappeared without a trace. I don't recall ever being told why she left but we accepted it as the way of things. An amah was only a servant, after all, and a master could rid himself of a servant with no recourse or questions asked. It was all rather feudal. I recall a conversation at the time between my parents to the effect that Ah Moy had some Communist literature (a pamphlet or flyer of some sort) that my mother had seen and told my father about.

The idea that Ah Moy could be a Communist would have been intolerable. I'm assuming my father dismissed her immediately, which wouldn't have been problematic because plenty of other amahs were looking for work. There's no one still living (not that I know of, that is) who can corroborate this story of her sacking, which admittedly gives me some latitude. Yet I think it's entirely possible it happened this way because across the colony there was an atmosphere of rebellion against this last outpost of imperial rule which was being played out in colonial Hong Kong. And there was a correlating paranoia about communism.

Local leftists had been taking advantage of the mounting discontent and seriously agitating since the middle of 1966. In December that year the troubles spread to Macau.

Whatever the reasons for her dismissal, Ah Moy – who had spent several years as a central figure in our daily life – was suddenly gone. Her replacement, Ah Lun, was a duller, far more traditional amah. Ah Moy had a little bit of style with her coloured suits and that chutzpah that marked her out as someone who worked as a servant without entirely seeing herself as one. She was certainly never servile. Ah Lun was a stolid woman with a round face, largely impassive except when watching Chinese opera. Then her visage became a twisted mask of misery. She was an amah by the numbers and wore the traditional black-and-white outfit that signified her role and social standing.

With limited English, she barely spoke to us kids. Mostly what I heard her say was "Yes Missy, yes Master". In the evenings, after dinner, she would take a break sitting in an ungainly fashion on the back steps, eating her own dinner and drinking hot water from a rice bowl.

When she took control of the chickens that Chinese New Year's Day in 1967 we imagined that she would take them out the back and pen them up somewhere. There was plenty of room for them. My brother, my sister and I were excited by the idea of having a little coop for our pet chickens and imagined we would now have a steady supply of eggs.

Ah Lun had other ideas.

After his morning audience with the staff, my father took us to the KCC for lunch. When we came back in mid-afternoon we were shocked to find Ah Lun had butchered, plucked and gutted the chooks, all in the space of a few hours. It was a shocking moment and, though I think my mother and father knew it might happen and that a chicken coop would not suit our lifestyle, they too seemed a little taken aback. The rear terrace, with its rows of pretty pot plants, had been turned into a charnel house, the concrete splattered with blood, gizzards and feathers. We were mortified and my sister shed some tears, but steadfast Ah Lun seemed pleased with herself and couldn't understand the fuss.

"I make good dinner," she assured us. "*See yao gai*" (soy sauce chicken).

Ah Lun had collected the giblets and put them in a bowl ready to cook for her own meal. I felt sick.

In ancient Rome they might have used those entrails for the purpose of divination and if any seer had been on hand he might have detected forebodings in the spray of chicken remains that Ah Lun soon hosed into a back gutter. Chinese New Year is a time to celebrate peace and prosperity and things seemed rosy enough after a few blips. As one of my father's English friends had put it, the natives were restless – but surely Britannia's rule could not be challenged.

Nobody could have foreseen the shadow that was about to fall across all our lives.

Terrible things were already happening in China, we knew that much, and the Cultural Revolution – unleashed by Mao in collaboration with Defence Minister Lin Biao and Mao's evil wife Jiang Qing, who went over the heads of other party leaders – had already opened the gates of hell. By the Chinese New Year when chickens in Kowloon Tong were having their necks wrung, a far greater bloodletting – of the human substance – was well under way to our north.

The bodies had already begun to arrive in Victoria Harbour. Australian poet Kenneth Slessor had written about '*convoys of dead sailors*' in his World War II poem *Beach Burial.* Quarter of a century on, the convoys of dead arriving in Hong Kong waters were civilians, washed down through the Pearl River Delta after executions across the border. An increase in sharks in the harbour was attributed to these victims of the Cultural Revolution. Not long after our Chinese New Year celebrations Uncle Cyril had reported to my father that several bloated corpses had floated into the construction works on a harbourside wharf they were building and that the horrified, highly superstitious workmen were pushing those bodies back out into the water with poles. One of the corpses was headless and the hands of many had been tied behind their backs.

The Cultural Revolution was an excuse for the summary execution of anyone deemed to be against the Communists.

It was assumed that Little Lee was a casualty of this mass brutality. Like Ah Moy he had disappeared. This seemed to be the year for it.

Little Lee had come to Hong Kong as a refugee from the mainland and fallen in with the imperialists, working for my father for several years. He was some sort of subcontractor, I guess, and my father held him in high regard. He had gone home to China just after Christmas 1966 to visit his dying mother even though that was a dangerous gambit considering what was going on. Chinese are big on filial piety – it's one of the central principles of Confucianism, which still underpins Chinese society today – and reverence for parents is important. It was particularly risky for someone who was by now something of a paper tiger himself: nevertheless he ventured north.

He was supposed to be away a week. One week turned into two, extended to a month, and eventually Chinese New Year came and went without his glistening presence. We never saw or heard from him again.

One evening I heard my father and Uncle Cyril discussing his disappearance as they propped up the bar in Kowloon Tong. They seemed certain that Little Lee, the man with the golden smile, had met his doom at the hands of the Red Guards who had been mobilised by Mao Tse-tung and his cronies to refresh his bloody revolution. That revolution turned into an excuse for bloodletting that would culminate in the violent deaths of at least 3 million people.

The disappearance of Little Lee was just one of a litany of bad omens that could have been read in those chicken entrails that cool day in early February 1967.

The Star Ferry Riots of 1966 had made it clear that Hong Kong's role as a sanctuary for people escaping communism in China was no guarantee that everyone granted such sanctuary would behave as docile subjects of colonial rulers. Those riots and the attempted burglary of our house at Kowloon Tong had disturbed our little idyll but the ripples from those stones dropped into our metaphorical pond dissipated in time and we carried on as if nothing was really wrong.

I entered my last term at KJS happy in my little English world. I continued to indulge my pop obsession and as the Summer of Love approached I had only one thing on my mind and it wasn't Mao Tse-tung but The Beatles' next album. For me the arrival of *Sgt. Pepper's Lonely Hearts Club Band* would be bigger than the Second Coming and was certainly more momentous than the Cultural Revolution.

Pop music was my religion, The Beatles its high priests and the pop press – functioning as the publishers of scriptural commentaries – was churning out article after article that got fans such as me in a lather.

I was waiting for the album's release when the real troubles began. It was on May 6, a few weeks before the release of *Sgt. Pepper's*, that a labour dispute flared at an artificial flower factory in the San Po Kong quarter of Kowloon. Picketing workers clashed with management and a riot broke out. Police were called and the violence spread.

Following that, large-scale demonstrations were held on crowded Hong Kong streets and pro-Communist demonstrators turned up waving their bible – *Quotations from Chairman Mao Tse-tung* or, as it was more commonly known in the West, *The Little Red Book* – the same little red book my father had on his bar, the one he was so fond of lampooning. His copy was the first English-language edition, published in 1966 just prior to the troubles.

The leftists were making all sorts of demands, including the unthinkable – overthrow of the British and the head of the Governor, a tall genial Englishman by the name of Sir David Trench. I have a photo of him with my father and in that picture the Governor is wearing a natty suit. I prefer to remember him in all his gubernatorial splendour – white uniform and hat adorned with ostrich-feather plumage.

On May 18 there was a confrontation outside Government House on Hong Kong Island. In *The Times*, foreign correspondent David Bonavia wrote: 'The worlds of Somerset Maugham and Mao Tse-tung met face to face in Hong Kong today. Both were baffled. Long before sundown the tumult and shouting died, and on balance it was a draw with points in favour of Maugham.'

That was certainly not the end of the matter as the troubles simmered and then exploded in the months to come. In stately Kowloon Tong we were largely oblivious to all this in the same way that – in the beginning at least – Marie Antoinette, cosseted at Versailles, was remote and unconcerned about the revolution brewing on her doorstep.

We could hardly imagine that a few kilometres away the Cultural Revolution was now raging on the streets of Kowloon and across the harbour on Hong Kong Island.

Despite that, I was still free to roam the streets between

bouts of civil strife and began haunting the record shop in Mody Rd, awaiting the arrival of *Sgt. Pepper's*. I remember the day in early June when it turned up at the store: I walked in and saw it being used as a kind of wallpaper by the enthusiastic proprietor. Obviously as excited as I was, he had placed copies of the album all round the shelves so that it surrounded you in all its colourful glory.

I can still recall that new LP smell and feel the excitement. When I got home I studied the cover and its plethora of personalities, including those wax figures of the Fab Four, and I played it over and over again on the little record player in my room. I experienced a kind of pop satori. It was psychedelic, lyrical, exotic (George Harrison's sitar playing on *Within You Without You* was other-worldly) and what a finale, the crescendo of *A Day in the Life*. Has a better pop song ever been written? Besides Procol Harum's *A Whiter Shade of Pale*, of course.

That album was the soundtrack of my last weeks at Kowloon Junior School as spring turned into summer. And it was the soundtrack that accompanied the months ahead, the time I refer to as the Summer of Discontent, which ran parallel to the Summer of Love. While the latter played out on the streets of Haight Ashbury in San Francisco, where everyone wore flowers in their hair, our summer erupted on the streets of Hong Kong, where plastic flowers and, as time went on, floral tributes held a darker significance.

This, Dad suggested, was precisely the sort of trouble that my grandfather had predicted, the reason he had quit the colony in 1951 and moved the family and the family business to Australia.

Grandad Bob was paranoid about the Communists taking

Hong Kong. The rest of us knew that would never happen. The Communist Chinese would never attack our world. Until they did.

On July 8, 1967 armed villagers from the People's Republic attacked a border police post at Sha Tau Kok, killing five policemen. Reports of uniformed people moving towards a major crossing point in force sent the colony into a panic. Britain's crack Nepalese troops, the Gurkhas, renowned for their tenacity and bravery in battle, were called in to secure the border. Five hundred soldiers from the 10th Gurkha Rifles, led by Major General Ronald McAlister, ended the siege of the police station and protected the border throughout the troubles. They were tough. I know because we used to play their children at soccer and even the kids were tough. We doubled up our shin pads for those matches.

The Cold War appeared to be heating up, lit by the flame of the Cultural Revolution, and for a brief time it threatened to engulf Hong Kong.

With the border secured, the leftists turned to terrorist bombings and that sent everyone into a panic. For the first time my parents looked worried and curfews were imposed to keep people off the streets and out of danger.

On August 20, at North Point on Hong Kong Island, two small children were killed by a bomb explosion, and four days later Cam Bun, a popular anti-leftist radio announcer, was murdered when petrol was doused on his car and set alight.

The death toll of police and civilians climbed and one of the most horrific deaths seemed all the more so to us because we watched it play out before our eyes, albeit at a very safe distance.

From our front yard in Kowloon Tong we had a perfect view of Lion Rock, towering in the distance, the most regal of Kowloon's eight hills. In late August bombs were placed at the summit along with a Chinese flag, and a British Army bomb disposal expert was called in to defuse them. We knew this was going on from radio reports and so were out in the garden with my father's binoculars trying to see what was happening. Here was a real-life drama and we were treating it like some spectator sport until eventually my mother, sensing something terrible might come of it, shut that down and called us all inside.

Later we heard that a sapper with the Royal Army Ordnance Corps had been killed in the operation, blown more than 60 metres down a cliff by the bomb he was trying to disable.

We were all shocked to the core.

After that we weren't sure if we would all be able to stay in Hong Kong but the troubles soon began to subside – although at a very high cost. By October, 51 people had been killed and more than 800 wounded. Hong Kongers had been given a taste of the Cultural Revolution on their own doorstep and it wasn't pleasant. Strangely, in December, Chinese Premier Zhou Enlai ordered leftist groups in Hong Kong to stop all their activities. Zhou was probably playing the long game, as the Chinese have so often done. He knew that his people had only to wait twenty years – a short time in the broad sweep of Chinese history – before Hong Kong would be China's again.

Today the troubles of 1967 are largely forgotten and unknown to many.

But we lived mostly normal lives throughout them and towards the end of our Summer of Discontent I walked up the long stairway from KJS to King George V School to begin my secondary education. I went with the songs of my latest acquisition ringing in my ears. I had just bought The Doors' new LP entitled, rather appropriately, *Strange Days*.

CHAPTER 13

THE DISHONOURABLE SCHOOLBOY

His voice was cultured but insistent. "Pay attention, Brown!" It was not the first time I had heard this. Mr Roberts was form master of 1A and we liked him because he cracked jokes and wore wildly colourful paisley ties in an era when paisley was king.

It wasn't just in his class that I was getting told to pay attention. Ever since arriving at King George V School (everyone just calls it KGV, pronounced K-G-5) for the Christmas term of 1967 I had been in trouble. I hadn't exactly been an angel at KJS but I did do well there. Looking back, I think my school results and success tended to track along with the teaching. If I liked and respected a teacher I did well. If there was a problem, well, that was reflected in my marks and behaviour.

In Miss Fung's Year 5 class, for example, I did OK yet could have done better. Miss Fung was prickly and there was some sort of disconnect. I would use the word 'frisson' if it weren't so pretentious.

In Year 6, under the tutelage of my class teacher, Mrs

Bramwell, I had excelled. So when I went up the long stairway to KGV I was put immediately into the A-stream, 1A. And I thought I was in good company. Mark Reeve, one of my closest mates, was also in that class. Mark was one of four brothers and one of them, Dermot, went on to play cricket for England before becoming a much loved cricket commentator and coach.

Now Mark Reeve was, and is, a great bloke but the two of us together were problematic. Not for *us*, you understand – for our teachers. We would sit near the back of the class and attempt to enjoy ourselves to relieve the utter boredom of whatever lesson it happened to be. Often when I was caught out I was responding to something Reevesy had done.

So when Mr Roberts called out "Pay attention, Brown!" what he should have said was: "Pay attention, Brown and Reeve!" How could I pay attention sitting next to Reevesy? One day someone had their pecker out down the back of the class. Reevesy swears it wasn't him. Whoever it was it caused quite a ruckus and Reevesy was in hysterics. When I joined in and laughed out loud, of course I'm the one who got into strife while Reevesy sat there relatively immune with a big grin on his cheeky freckled face.

That seemed to set a pattern for how things would run for me at KGV. I was at the school for only two years, but they were two of the most significant of my life. I haven't managed to make the famous-alumni list, however, and have been checking it for years. Michael Hutchence is on it, as he should be, although I was a year or two ahead of him; and the author Martin Booth is there of course. He wrote the acclaimed Hong Kong memoir *Gweilo*, which I read with some trepidation.

It's so revered that it nearly put me off writing my own story. Nearly. And Dermot Reeve is on the list, along with some judges and other notables.

KGV has a special place in the colonial history of Hong Kong. Its earliest iteration was Kowloon College, established in 1894 on Nathan Rd to cater for the children of British people living in Kowloon, which was still regarded as a den of iniquity. That first school was destroyed by a typhoon. (As kids in Hong Kong we loved typhoons because school was often closed down whenever one was approaching.) In KGV's earlier incarnations it had gone through a number of name changes. At one stage it was the Kowloon British School, then Central British School, and later, finally, King George V School. It was relocated to its present site at Ho Man Tin, mid-Kowloon, in 1936. When the Japanese invaded China and Europeans fled south to Hong Kong (the Browns among them) the school became a refugee camp. Then when the Europeans were evacuated it became an army hospital, and during the Japanese occupation it was a hospital for POWs.

As soon as the war was over the Union Jack was hoisted again and the school was revived as a bastion of Britishness in one of the last outposts of Empire.

During my two years at KGV I lived a real-life version of *Goodbye Mr Chips* with a touch of *Lord of the Flies* thrown in for good measure. That air of Britishness was all-pervasive.

It's strange to me that my father eschewed our Englishness because I have always embraced it. I felt quite British as a schoolboy in Hong Kong although I was always singled out as Australian. There were a few Aussies in 1A, including my friend Timothy Budge, (or Budgie as we called him). Budgie,

Reevesy and I played cricket together at KGV and I have a wonderful team photo taken for the school magazine, *The Lion* (the school's symbol is a rampant British lion), that shows us all in white looking quite serious.

I loved cricket and watched as much as I could when there were matches on at the KCC. Was I any good at it? Not really. I was rather a nervous player and terrified of facing some of the Indian boys who bowled too fast for my liking. I would occasionally field at silly mid-on, holding my hands up in front of my face so as not to get hit with the ball. My batting was defensive in the extreme. Yet I loved it and one of my strongest memories of Hong Kong at that time is the smell of linseed oil which I used to condition my bat. I would sit out on the front terrace at home in Kowloon, transistor by my side, as I lovingly rubbed oil into my cricket bat like some attentive massage therapist.

I also played soccer and had begun playing at Kowloon Junior School. We were bussed all over the colony for games. If our toughest opponents were those Gurkha children, the regular British Army kids were also pretty rough.

I played at left half and was, again, mediocre although I had occasional flashes of brilliance. Reevesy and my friend Greg England were much better at soccer and I remember Greg's skills in particular. Greg went missing for half a year after we first went up to KGV and I discovered only recently that he and his family came to Australia to live for six months. Bizarrely enough they lived in Brisbane, just near where I live now. Greg turned up a few months after we'd already started at KGV and he came into 1A with us.

Sometimes we'd all play soccer at lunchtime and captains

would pick sides, I remember being embarrassed on several occasions because I was always the last person picked.

At one time I considered playing rugby and went to a big meeting where we were all gathered in a big auditorium and given a very British rundown on the rugby program. It was like a scene from Hogwarts, all of us boys in blazers and the master shouting, "I say, you lads, settle down now." I half-heartedly attended a trial match but didn't put my hand up to go any further. I mean, my God, I could have got hurt!

My cowardice disappointed Dad. He had played rugby for Hong Kong after the war and still had cauliflower ears to show for it. I have an album full of photos and newspaper clippings about his glory days playing for the Hong Kong Football Club. From rugby hero to rugby zero in one generation.

I did better at track and field, though, and wasn't too shabby in the swimming stakes either. I was in Crozier House and still have some photos of me competing on house sports days.

We often played sport at lunchtime too, after visiting the canteen, which was run by a Chinese lady called Suzie. She ran that canteen for years and everyone in the KGV diaspora remembers her well.

I loved the soft white bread we got at lunch, a touch sweet in the Chinese fashion, with crispy crusts and excellent bangers with gravy. All this washed down with chocolate milk.

KGV was a little world unto itself. Let me show you round. Out front were the sports fields, surrounded by a grassy mound behind which we used to gather for our nefarious activities. At one point we had a poker school going on at lunchtime there, gambling for piffling sums and smoking all the while. The field itself was said to have been built over the graves of people who died under the Japanese occupation, and the cricket pavilion used as a torture chamber, though neither rumour was ever confirmed.

The pavilion was another of our hangouts, and behind it I was shown pornography for the first time by a boy who is, I believe, now a well-known Hong Kong barrister. I was a bit naïve, not to say confused, and couldn't quite make out what was what going on in the magazines he showed us in secret there.

We would also smoke there, out of sight.

Our class was in a new block separated from the older part of the school by a covered walkway. After traversing the walkway you would pass the prefects' room and I always looked in the window to see the poster of Mao Tse-tung they had on the wall there with a hole cut into it and a real cigarette dangling from the lips. This was to belittle the dictator and yet was curiously appropriate because Mao was a heavy smoker. And apparently he had bad breath and terrible body odour.

There was a patch of ground between the buildings where we used to play hockey and football. Once, when it was a tad wet underfoot, we got into a bit of a mud fight there which landed us in all sorts of trouble.

I remember being called out of class and lined up in the corridor like motley troops. It was like a scene from *It Ain't Half Hot Mum* and the sergeant major was none other than Reevesy's dad, the deputy headmaster, who inspected us with the disdain of a real sergeant major and asked us all what the hell we thought we were playing at. When we told him, that didn't go down well either so we were sent to the headmaster,

Mr Gore, a somewhat rotund man who spoke in cultured, measured tones. In the school song at assembly he led us like some kind of genial bishop.

Honestas Ante Honores was our motto and the title of the school song. It's Latin, of course, and means … Honesty before Glory. I'd know more about Latin if I'd been at KGV earlier. In fact I had Latin textbooks for my first year there but they cancelled the teaching of Latin just as I arrived at the school. Standing in the historic assembly hall with the music swelling and the school body singing *Honestas Ante Honores*, I felt part of something bigger than myself, a tradition that I embraced.

The school motto and song bind together the KGV diaspora and I was horrified to find out recently that *Honestas Ante Honores* has been all but ditched and replaced with *Be Your Own Remarkable*, which is as lame as it is pretentious. I have heard that the current student body is as disgusted as the diaspora, and a friend in Hong Kong and former KGV'er tells me the English Schools Foundation which now runs the school is even thinking of changing its name. That would be a travesty and tantamount to sacrilege as far as I'm concerned.

Avuncular Mr Gore wouldn't have stood for that. I have fond memories of Mr Gore: getting sent to him wasn't that scary and, though I fully expected to be caned for my part in the infamous mud fight, I was instead punished by having to stand outside his office with my co-conspirators over several lunch hours.

Reevesy and I were often in trouble together, although he was no slouch at getting into trouble all by himself. The most famous example of that was when he scrawled some graffiti on a drawing of Jesus that was hanging in the foyer near the office. He was from a strongly Catholic household so maybe that was his way of rebelling. What he scrawled shocked everyone although it was fairly pithy. It simply said: FUCK OFF.

It was one of the major dramas of my time at KGV.

Another was when some students and parents, who were out on a boat in the waters off Hong Kong's ragged coastline, were captured by a Chinese gunboat and held in Communist China. The school was assembled to be informed of this and to pray for the people involved. I remember it well because Tim Budge's sister, Jocelyn, was among those abducted. They were held on the mainland for about six weeks, then released just in time for Jocelyn to attend a performance of the musical *Oliver!* starring Tim in the title role.

Our class, though largely Anglo-Celtic, included Americans, Canadians and some Scandinavians. There was a girl by the name of Sarah von Sydow whose uncle was the acclaimed Swedish actor Max von Sydow. There was only one Chinese person in our class, Elizabeth See ('See See'), who had come up with us from KJS. There was a Eurasian guy named Douglas Board who was basically a genius and the smartest kid in our year. We called his parents 'Toothpick' and '*Wah Mui*' because his father was tall and skinny, and his mother short (not because she looked like a dried plum).

Our teachers were all British and most were nice, though I didn't much care for my physics teacher, Mr Hackling. He humiliated me in front of the class one day, just because I had been doing an X-rated drawing rather than concentrating on my work. In one of my father's girlie magazines I'd seen a rude yet very amusing cartoon that I was trying to replicate on a sheet of notepaper for Reevesy when I was told to bring it out the front, which I duly did. Mr Hackling asked me to show him it and, seeing that it was of an unsavoury nature, he slapped it out of my hand.

Not nice but that was typical of how things were starting to go for me at KGV. It's hard to know exactly why I was going off the rails. Did it have anything to do with what was going on at home? Perhaps.

I mean, despite our having a happy family life I was increasingly aware of tension between my parents over Dad's drinking. My unruly behaviour at school may have been related to that. Or was it just because I was an immature adolescent boy?

My report card is in front of me as I write and if you made a graph relating my results to my behaviour in that first year at KGV (1967-68) it would resemble the stock market crash of 1929. While there are a few scribblings of 'Satisfactory' most of the comments are negative. For geography in the Christmas term of 1967 it read, 'Disappointing standard'. For history, 'A disappointing result'.

At the end of that page the headmaster, Mr Gore, has written, 'Sorry that this result means a transfer to 1B next term.' He didn't carry through on that immediately: I remained in 1A as things went from bad to worse. For the maths subjects in Easter term the comment reads, 'More attention needed during lessons, Phillip is easily distracted.'

Our form master, Mr Roberts, he of the paisley ties, gave a withering assessment of 'Below A-stream standard' for that term and the bastard wrote 'No different' at the end of summer term.

The headmaster, not to be outdone, wrote at length, 'I have seldom to comment on the behaviour of A-stream students in class but Phillip is proving a disturbing influence and he is seriously being considered for demotion because of this.'

For all Mr Gore's likeness to an uncle, maybe he was a bastard too.

Still they kept me in A-stream for one more term, through to Christmas 1968, before I was demoted to 2B. I don't remember feeling terribly upset about this, and Greg England was demoted with me so I had company. He tells me his six months in Brisbane had unsettled him – and six months in Brisbane in 1967 would have unsettled anyone, I reckon.

My memories of 2B are hazy. I know there was a rather sweet Canadian girl called Kate in the class and it turns out she had a crush on me. This affection expressed itself openly at the school's annual Spring Fair. They had a sort of mock jail where people were locked up after being reported by someone and then payment had to be made for their release, all a bit of fun. Kate arranged for me to be banged up as a way of getting my attention and I remember shouting at her because I was annoyed and embarrassed. I was really cruel to her but, hell, I was only twelve.

I did well in 2B and really well in English thanks to my teacher, a rather brusque Englishwoman called Miss Hesketh. She was tough but terrific. She basically took me by the scruff of the neck, shook me and inspired me to work hard, if just to impress her. I topped the class of thirty-four students in English. Demotion had kick-started me again, which may have been what they were hoping for.

It was all too late because that summer term was my last.

I'm looking at the report card now and it reads: 'Next term commences Sept 8th, 1969.'

By then I would be in another hemisphere.

An abiding KGV memory is of a mendicant or hermit, if those are acceptable terms, who used to live in a little cave on the side of the hill nearby. I wrote a poem about this memory entitled *The Hermit*, which goes like this:

Near my school
Was a hill of red earth
Where an old hermit lived.
We skirted it carefully
Each afternoon
Going to our homes.
He threw rocks
From a distance
And cursed us. …
We laughed and went away singing …
The stones fell short at our backs
And his curses
Melted into tears.

It was a poetic memory yet I was never sure if it was true. Then, one day, I was in a taxi in Brisbane. I could detect from the driver's accent that he was a Hong Konger and we got chatting.

It turned out that as a young man he'd lived not far from KGV and without any prompting he asked me if I remembered the angry man who lived in the cave just near the school. I told him I did and was amazed that he knew of the man who lived like a ragged beggar in a hole on the side of the hill just outside the grounds of a school for privileged Westerners. Thinking from my enlarged understanding of the world what that life must have been like, no wonder he was angry.

CHAPTER 14

ROCK STAR ACROSS THE ROAD

When I knew Michael Hutchence only one of us had ever fronted a band and it wasn't him. My time as co-lead singer of The Sidetracks was a flash in the pan, admittedly, but I had one up on him. Now I'm not saying I'm the guy responsible for turning the future frontman of INXS onto pop music. Let me just add, I'm not saying I wasn't either. Because I might well have been.

The fact of the matter is I was the cool guy with the record player, the collection of Beatles records and the Jimi Hendrix poster on my bedroom wall. And Michael was the younger kid from across the road who may – or may not – have looked up to me as a rock god.

In the late Sixties the Hutchence family lived directly opposite us in Kowloon Tong. They lived on Hong Kong side originally, decamping to Australia during the troubles in mid-1967 and coming back to settle in Kowloon Tong when things had died down.

Michael and his little brother Rhett, who was a bit of a tearaway, spent a lot of time at our place along with the other kids in the neighbourhood. The Hutchence boys went to Beacon Hill School at that stage and Michael eventually went on to KGV, following in my footsteps. They had an older sister, Tina, who by then was back in Australia.

She was working as a buyer for the Sportsgirl boutique chain but rejoined the family in Hong Kong in late 1968. Tina lived briefly in Kowloon Tong but was nearly 21 by then and didn't hang out with us kids.

Our palace compound, as I like to refer to it, was Kowloon Tong's Fun Central and 7 Devon Rd was its own little world where play wars raged, music played and cricket matches were staged in the spacious front yard. My sister Jane's Russian friend, Margarita Ivanchenko, could often be found there. She lived down the street and her father was this huge Russian bear of a bloke called Nick. The girls used to don their white go-go boots and practise their dancing up and down the front pathway while we made fun of them. Pop music blared from my transistor, and Michael and Rhett were there most afternoons.

The girls were sweet on Michael, of course, something I don't think I realised at the time. In fact it was only recently that my sister divulged to me that she had been in love with Michael Hutchence. She probably wasn't the first and certainly wouldn't be the last.

At one stage the Hutchence boys virtually lived at our place. I guess they liked us but there was another reason. My mother told me once that they had a very strict old cook amah, Ah Chang, who wouldn't allow them in her kitchen after school. I had a conversation with Tina Hutchence about this recently and she said that everyone was afraid of Ah Chang.

Their mother, Patricia Hutchence – Pat to all of us – was often at work so they came over to our place seeking company and snacks, as well as to escape their glowering amah. Their father, Kell, worked for some sort of trading company that had an office in Kowloon and a factory in the New Territories. We didn't see much of him.

Pat was a lovely lady and quite glamorous in our eyes because she worked in the movie business. She was a make-up artist. Michael and Rhett raided her make-up kit and shared fake blood capsules with us, which we put to good use scaring the hell out of my mother. Pat Hutchence did some work for the famous Shaw Brothers studios which had been founded in 1958 and produced romantic films, martial arts flicks and historical epics. One of my favourites – which I didn't see until many years later in Australia, by which time it was a cult classic – was *One-Armed Swordsman*, made in 1967. I went to see it in the Cinémathèque at the Gallery of Modern Art in Brisbane a couple of years ago and it still holds up. Shaw Brothers under Sir Run Run Shaw, as he would later become – he was the youngest of the brothers behind the business and lived to the age of 106 – was pumping out movies on a production line by the mid-Sixties and was largely responsible for turning Hong Kong into the Hollywood of the Chinese world.

The local industry had already given a young actor called Bruce Lee his start and he would go on to make a name for himself in America, eventually returning to Hong Kong and worldwide fame as the star of *Enter the Dragon*. By which time he would be dead. Lee actually lived in Kowloon Tong, moving there not long after we left. And they used to say he died there too, in 1973, although it has been revealed recently that he didn't die at home in Cumberland Rd as first reported, he died in his mistress's apartment at Beacon Hill just a stone's throw from Devon Rd, near where the Hutchence boys went to primary school. Knowing that I lived in the same suburb as Bruce Lee has always appealed to me. Kowloon Tong, I figured, was where rich successful people lived.

The famous Hong Kong actress Nancy Kwan also lived in Kowloon Tong and my father knew her as a girl because my grandfather was friendly with her dad, Honkie Kwan, who was an architect. Nancy went to Maryknoll Convent, the same school my aunties attended before World War II. She came to prominence in the 1960 movie *The World of Suzie Wong* starring alongside William Holden. When my father knew her she was only a girl: by the time we returned to Hong Kong in the Sixties she was a big name and maybe the first Chinese actress to crack Hollywood.

Kowloon Tong became so associated with glamour and celebrity that even the suburb itself became a star of the screen. With its quiet streets, laneways and impressive mansions it was an ideal location to shoot a movie relatively undisturbed. Occasionally we would come across film crews in the streets nearby. I was always struck by just how many people it took to do this because there would always be a crowd gathered, lots of people in sunglasses and others holding those big tin reflectors that glint in the sunlight. There was plenty of shouting in high-flown Cantonese until the filming started.

One day our amah went out to the front gate to let someone in and next thing we heard her scream "*Aiyah!*" We all came running outside to see what had happened. It must have been a holiday because we were all home from school. She had screamed as you would do if you opened your front gate and found a body lying in a pool of blood in the middle of the road right outside your house.

A film crew had decided to set up shop right outside 7 Devon Rd and the storyline of this particular movie was obviously some sort of dramatic murder scenario. We arrived breathless at the pavement to find Ah Lun talking to someone from the film crew who had obviously asked if we could all go back inside. Cheeky bugger. The least he could have done would be to offer us roles as extras because, I tell you, we were up for it. Anyway we shut the gate and let them get on with it. I climbed up into the tree that abutted our front wall and overhung the street, the ideal vantage point to watch the scene being shot. It seemed to take forever and when it was done they hosed away the blood and departed, leaving no sign they had ever been there.

The Hutchences' address was 5 Dorset Crescent – as I said, directly opposite us, at the point where Dorset Cres., which comes off Kowloon Tong's main artery of Waterloo Rd, meets Devon Rd. There was a bit of serendipity involved in this address because that house happened to be the Brown family residence in the post-war glory days when the family was living the high life. It was quite incredible to me that it had been my father's home and now we lived just across the road, but Dad wasn't particularly sentimental about it.

He only told us a couple of stories about his time living there and both involved road accidents. One recalled a night when he drove a car home from The Peninsula bouncing off the walls of the *nullah* (a huge stone-walled drain) that ran down the middle of Waterloo Rd. The other involved a motorbike he'd bought in his twenties. The first day he rode it he drove out his front gate at Dorset Cres., gunned the accelerator, roared across the road and smashed into the wall of 7 Devon Rd, where we lived all those years later. Thus ended the great motorbike experiment.

Although the Hutchence boys spent a lot of time at our house, occasionally we did go over to theirs and whenever we did I tried to imagine their house full of Browns as it would have been in the 1940s. On one visit it got a bit weird because their mum got out this Ouija board for contacting the spirit world. We tried to conjure up some entities and commune with the great beyond – to no avail, thank God. I've always been a bit of a scaredy-cat about such things and figure the spirit world should be left alone.

One day we were summoned to the Hutchences to meet a friend of Pat's from Australia, the actor Reg Gorman, whom everyone would eventually know as Jack Fletcher in *The Sullivans*. Pat had met him working for Crawford Productions back in Australia.

We had no idea who he was, only that he'd been on television – and that was enough to impress us. Our admiration turned into adulation as Reg did impressions to entertain us. His Daffy Duck was quite brilliant, I recall, and we all fell about laughing at him.

Mostly the Hutchence boys were at our place. After raiding the kitchen we would all rampage around the grounds playing war games or ping-pong on a table set up in the front yard or swinging on the Tarzan rope we had attached to a big jacaranda over by the fence. The old Chinese lady who lived on one side would always shout out in Cantonese for us to shut up (we got the gist) but we ignored her. If Dad was home he would shout back at her, also in Cantonese. She didn't hold with noisy *gweilos* disturbing her Kowloon Tong idyll.

Sometimes we would just hang out on the front porch, a stone affair with steps that led down into the garden. Two throne-like peacock chairs sat either side of the French doors. Here I would play my transistor which blared out music by The Beatles, The Doors, Cream, the Stones and other stuff that was top of the pops. I wonder now: was Michael soaking up my music even then for later reference? Occasionally I would bring down records from my room and put them on Mum and Dad's Grundig radiogram which sat in the front room that led onto the porch.

I have a few photos of Michael from that time, one on a boat which means he must have come with us to the beach one day. We used to go to a spot called Hebe Haven, also known as Pak Sha Wan, literally 'White Sand Bay', which is on the south shore of Sai Kung Peninsula in the eastern part of the New Territories. Hebe is the Greek goddess of youth, daughter of Zeus and Hera. To get to Hebe Haven we had to catch a sampan that would drop us at the beach and pick us up a few hours later. There's a photo of Michael, me and my brother Steve perched at the prow of one of those rickety little vessels.

There are also a couple of photos of the Hutchence boys at my brother's birthday party which was held in the front yard. His birthday is in February so it was cool and Michael Hutchence is standing there wearing a jumper and white turtleneck underneath. He's holding a bottle of Green Spot – a popular soft drink from those times, not the Irish whiskey, for which we were a bit young – and staring straight at the camera (which, I'm assuming, my father was holding) with a big grin on his face. The camera loved him even then, and he loved it right back. But if you had stood us side by side in the late Sixties and assessed either of us for future rock stardom I probably would have come out on top. I mean, I had already been in a band and I dressed the part with my suede shoes, Beatle boots, paisley shirts and slim-fit jeans with my hair brushed down Fab Four-style.

After we left Hong Kong in late 1969 the Hutchences stayed on for a couple more years. We lost touch with them as we did with most of the people we had known in Hong Kong. Even though I have no idea who moved into 7 Devon Rd after we left I'm guessing things there were never quite the same as when we lived there.

Just over a decade later Michael came onto my radar again although I had heard of him in the meantime. Mainly because his family moved back to Sydney and lived at Belrose behind Sydney's northern beaches: my cousins lived in the same suburb and were enrolled, as he was, at nearby Davidson High School.

One day in 1981 my cousin Peter, Uncle Cyril's son, was visiting us on the Gold Coast and we all sat down for the ritual watching of *Countdown* when this band came on with a young foppish Mick Jagger type gyrating out front, flopping his hair around. He was like Jagger and Jim Morrison rolled into one. The song was *The Loved One*. The band was INXS.

"They're pretty cool," I said.

"You know who that is?" my cousin Peter asked.

"No, who?"

"That's bloody Michael Hutchence." I looked more closely and even went over to the TV to inspect him. And yes, I could see it *was* Michael. I was astounded yet, instead of being thrilled, my initial reaction was typically self-absorbed. I thought … *Wait a minute, that should be me!* Eventually his mum, Pat, came to live on the Gold Coast where she worked for the movie studios. She was still doing movie make-up. My mum caught up with her to talk about Hong Kong days. Dad had died and that made Hong Kong memories special, if at times painfully poignant. Some time later I went to have coffee with Pat and showed her my photo album that included those pictures of her boys at our place in Kowloon Tong. She was a lovely lady.

A few years after that I was in a café at the swanky Marina Mirage shopping mall on The Spit at Main Beach just north of Surfers Paradise when I spotted Pat and Michael Hutchence walking past. I rushed out to say hello. And Michael seemed genuinely blown away to see me. He had a lifelong love of Hong Kong and returned there often. Like mine, his Hong Kong childhood was a sort of spiritual touchstone. We had that special bond because we'd been kids there together and had such happy memories of those days in the yard at Kowloon Tong. Of course now he was a big star but he was no poser. He was friendly and chatty and we gabbed on about Honkers. And as we stood there a small crowd began to form around the edge of our conversation.

He'd been spotted. I apologised for drawing attention to his presence but he was cool. He thought he'd been hiding behind his sunglasses but there was no mistaking Michael Hutchence. I shook hands, excused myself, and he and his mum walked off although he turned and blew a kiss to the little group that had gathered to worship him.

A couple of years later my brother caught up with him in Vancouver. Steve, who had been a cop back on the Gold Coast, works as a private investigator in the Canadian city where he still lives with his wife, Kelly. (They have two grown-up children, my niece and nephew Chelsea and Nicholas.) He presented himself backstage at the concert and Michael got the message that Stephen Brown from 7 Devon Rd, Kowloon Tong, was there and ushered him backstage to meet the band. Such were the perks of knowing Michael.

He was a lovely kid. I mean I didn't have a crush on him even if all the girls in Kowloon Tong seemed to. Maybe some of the boys did too, though I couldn't say.

What happened to him is really beyond words to express. When he died so tragically in 1997 I was, like everyone else, devastated. He was so young and talented, and it was just so sad.

I'm looking at that picture of him in our Kowloon Tong garden even as I write. His little brother Rhett is busy looking at the birthday cake and my little brother Steve is busy blowing out the candles. Michael is looking straight at the camera and beaming as if he's the birthday boy. It's a smile etched in my memory and preserved in my photo album like the fading evidence of some lost civilisation.

CHAPTER 15

JET SET

Tony Parr may have been an engineer: to me he looked like a spy. This tall, smooth Englishman resembled two rather suave actors – the Canadian star Lloyd Bochner and the British actor (and former model) Roger Moore who wasn't yet in the frame to play James Bond back then. I was a huge Roger Moore fan and used to watch episodes of his show *The Saint* on the little TV in my room in Kowloon Tong. Moore was charming and debonair and drove around in sports cars with nary a hair out of place.

The signature, rather jazzy theme music from *The Saint* still casts its spell on me. I hear it and am immediately transported back to Kowloon Tong where I'm sitting high in a tree watching Tony Parr arrive at our house by taxi.

That tree was in a little traffic-island-cum-garden where Dorset Cres. and Devon Rd met. We used to climb up into it and heckle passers-by, hidden by the foliage. There was an American who wore garish Bermuda shorts and used to walk his dog by our house. Whenever he went past we would call out, "Hairy legs! Hairy legs!" from on high.

We were up our tree one day when I saw Tony Parr pull up and I recollect telling my pal – it could have been an English boy called Colin who lived nearby – that he was a spy. Tony Parr looked like one, or at least the Hollywood idea of one. He was tall, handsome, and wore natty suits with a sliver of white handkerchief peeking out of his jacket pocket.

A photo still in my possession – taken amid the tangle of steel and concrete on one of my father's building sites – shows Tony looking as if he has just stepped away from a cocktail party or a meeting with M at MI6. This was the era of Bond, after all, and as far as I was concerned Tony Parr looked closer to how James Bond should than Sean Connery did. The Bond movies were big in the mid-1960s and I remember the huge fuss when *Thunderball* came out. Back then my parents used to dress up to go to the cinema and I remember them going off to see *Thunderball* all dolled up. Not only would Tony have made a good Bond, he had a touch of the Pierce Brosnans about him too. And my fantasy about him being a spy wasn't entirely out of the question.

There were plenty of spies in Hong Kong in the Sixties, on both sides of the Cold War. My father always claimed to know a few of those spooks who drank at The Pen, though he never named names.

In my imagination Tony Parr was a British agent merely posing as an engineer working for an imperialist running dog (my dad) as cover. That would enable him to move freely around Hong Kong and keep an eye on the Communist cadres who might have infiltrated my father's workforce. In turn that would enable him to keep London fully briefed on what the Communists were up to. To me Tony Parr was a spy, I was sure of it.

Unless, of course, he was just an engineer. That was a much more boring prospect. Although I guess he did go through the motions of being an engineer. He was in charge of my father's business in Thailand, a partnership with a Thai company run by a woman who was reputedly the former mistress of a Japanese general during the gruelling occupation years of World War II.

This woman was wealthy and, to a point, charming. She was also ruthless and less inclined than some to rely on Western etiquette in business relations. My father was something of a handshake man and took people at their word. For a while his Bangkok-based company, Siam Foundations, looked like taking off and we all travelled to Bangkok when his business in Thailandwas in the ascendant. We stayed in a five-star hotel that was mainly memorable for serving amazing hamburgers. The Americans on R&R from Vietnam demanded American food and our hotel had the best hamburgers and fries we had ever eaten. When we were kids that kind of thing excited us more than the cultural highlights although we did our fair share of temple visits too and made the obligatory pop-in to the Royal Palace.

We also spent a few days down at the beachside resort of Pattaya, which was much less sleazy then than it is now. We drank coconut juice on the beach straight from the shell. My father's accountant, Harry King, and his family were on that trip with us and a scare involving them made our stay there unforgettable. The resort where we were staying had some free-ranging monkeys, one of which bit Gregory, the elder of Harry King's two sons. It was quite dramatic and he had to have rabies shots afterwards. Ever since then I have never trusted monkeys.

Tony Parr was in Bangkok as well, where he met my father

in the hotel and looked sharper than ever in a suit he had probably just had made in the Thai capital where Mum went mad over the Thai silk that was all the rage at the time.

Quite the ladies' man Tony was and, according to my mother, he played the field while in Thailand, took his eye off running the business and thus allowed my father's Thai partner to take him to the cleaners. Mum always blamed Tony Parr's love life for the fact that Dad's Thai business dealings went south.

Tony Parr was just one of the people who used to gather at our house in Kowloon Tong, often for cocktails, before a night on the town.

The crowd around the bar some evenings consisted of people who looked as though they had just stepped out of an episode of *Mad Men* or a cigarette commercial. At the time the cigarette brand Peter Stuyvesant was running ads showing the glamorous jet set living the high life in Hong Kong, which was dubbed the Pearl of the Orient. Peter Stuyvesant was, apparently, 'the international passport to smoking pleasure' and synonymous with that jet set. Smoking was part of social life back then and there was always a small cloud of smoke hanging over the bar at our house, particularly if my Uncle Cyril was around. He never had a cigarette out of his hand.

Tony Parr had a gold cigarette case with a gold lighter to match and used it to light the cigarettes of the ladies, an act of gallantry. Never mind the lung cancer.

Occasionally we had visitors from Australia over and I know on one occasion there was a young woman who was a friend of the family, a quite attractive blonde whom Tony Parr seemed to latch onto. In a box of family photos, among a series of nightclub snaps, there's one of them both. He has his arm around her and looks quite pleased with himself.

Nightclubs and restaurants all seemed to have photographers on hand in those times so I have a swag of pictures of Mum and Dad out living the high life while we were home with our amah. Whenever my parents left the house the amah would watch Chinese opera on the Chinese channel. Ah Lun was extremely demonstrative and from our bedrooms we could her sobbing and howling. Cantonese opera could be pretty tragic at times, it seemed. We could never understand the attraction when, coming and going from the kitchen, we would catch a bit of it in passing. It sounded like nothing short of caterwauling to us, caterwauling accompanied by the rattling of pots and pans in the background. All this in very elaborate costumes.

After watching this stuff, Ah Lun was emotionally drained, even visibly devastated.

My parents often presaged their evenings out with those small gatherings around the bar at home. As well as Tony Parr and my Uncle Cyril and Aunty Ruth, Harry King was sometimes there in his natty suits and hair slicked down with Brylcreem. To me he looked like a Mob accountant. His wife, Joyce, was a small woman whose face constantly wore a strained look and she was a chain-smoker. Other Australian friends were Don and Vera Williamson. Don was a fire chief in the colony who later went on to the equivalent position in the Australian Capital Territory. He specialised in industrial fires, which were a particular problem in Hong Kong with its plastics factories. In one respect Hong Kong then was the way mainland China is now: everything in the house seemed to be 'Made in Hong

Kong' and the factories employed a burgeoning population being perpetually topped up with refugees from the north.

Mum and Dad had some other English friends whose names I cannot remember, although I can recall their accents. They were from Yorkshire and you had only to hear their broad brogue to know that. My father had explained to them that they were exempt from his pathological hatred of Yorkshiremen. His sister Eileen had married a bloke from Yorkshire called Charles Tiernan, a philandering cad who put my father and his brothers off Yorkshiremen for life. With the exception of his two friends in Hong Kong.

Behind his bar in Kowloon Tong my father presided with ice tongs at the ready, clinking cubes into crystal glasses of Johnnie Walker Black Label Scotch whisky and doling out Pimm's No. 1 Cup, a popular tipple with the ladies.

They would sometimes all end up at our bar later in the evening, too, when we would be woken by loud voices and laughing. Dad would meet people in bars, at cocktail parties over dinner, and drag them home for a nightcap. On occasions he latched onto soldiers or sailors, Australians and Americans. He was extremely gregarious, which had its good and bad sides. He also drank too much, which was becoming more apparent as the years went by.

That said, he was in his element. My father loved Hong Kong and much of the time acted as if he owned the place. He had half the town's *maître d*'s (in Honkers they were referred to as 'captains') in his pocket. I was always amazed whenever we entered a restaurant because he would be greeted like a long-lost friend. The captain would drop everything to attend to him, welcoming him – and, by association, us – with open arms. After they shook hands we would be shown to the best table and treated like royalty. Of course that initial handshake usually contained some folded bills. Greasing palms oiled the machinery of our social life.

Money and familiarity worked in tandem because in some places the staff had been there since the Forties when my father and his family ruled their little kingdom from Kowloon Tong and were known in all the bars, restaurants and hotels of Kowloon.

At home Dad was the 'host with the most', dispensing more than just drinks. He was also known for his ability to spout Chairman Mao's gobbets of wisdom.

In 1966, as the Cultural Revolution gained momentum, Dad obtained a copy of '*The Little Red Book*', the reviled publication that was so dominant in the riots of 1967 when thousands of Communist cadres waved it fanatically during street demonstrations. I'm not sure if he had bought it himself or if someone had given it to him as a joke.

I still have that little book, with its plain red plastic cover, in my desk drawer. The leaves are yellowing now. A few pages in there's a picture of Mao preserved behind a thin film of tissue paper. He looks quite nice and genial but we all knew he was dangerous. The way my parents and their friends dealt with him was by ridiculing him. To them he was a vicious dictator *and* a figure of fun.

I recall the uproar Mao caused when he supposedly swam across the Yangtze River in the middle of 1966. He was 72 at the time and reportedly led 5000 adoring followers on an annual swim in Wuhan. It was regarded as one of the most powerful publicity stunts in Chinese history and it happened

– or was staged – just as the Cultural Revolution was being launched.

I recollect clearly the photo of Mao on the *South China Morning Post*'s front page. He was just a head bobbing in the water and everyone reckoned they had just stuck a photo of Mao's noggin onto another photo in a rudimentary form of early Photoshopping.

According to my parents, Mao was a buffoon and his purported swim was mercilessly lampooned. Having a copy of '*The Little Red Book*' on the bar may have seemed odd but it was mainly used as a kind of joke book and at times Dad would stand and read it like a priest intoning a liturgy: "Revolutions and revolutionary wars are inevitable in class society … The people's democratic dictatorship needs the leadership of the working class … There is a serious tendency towards capitalism among the well-to-do peasants." The well-to-do, assembled at my father's bar, laughed their heads off as he pilloried the great man.

Had my father been an American I don't think keeping *Quotations from Chairman Mao Tse-tung* on the bar would have been acceptable. Americans were pretty serious about communism, and among Yanks in Hong Kong at one stage there was an unspoken rule that when you drank a Scotch and water you always left a little in the glass in case the water might have come from Red China. The thought of that made them gag.

My dad had a lot of fun with his '*Little Red Book*' and called himself Chairman Ted as he read from it. I keep it in the top drawer of the old Chinese desk that I inherited when he passed away. Next to it is a sheaf of old Hong Kong prints and a battered copy of another little book, Y.C. Yuen's *A Guide to Cantonese (Self-taught)* which I dip into from time to time.

Occasionally my father's business partners would be among the guests around the bar at Kowloon Tong. His Hong Kong company, Brown & Godfrey Ltd, was a partnership with some Australian businessmen, the Godfreys. I can only recall the name of one of them because it happened to be Phil. And I remember him for all the wrong reasons.

First, he had a Chinese wife or girlfriend, one who didn't come from money – and that set him apart socially.

Second, he was ill. Very ill. Sicker than anyone imagined. He had cancer. Dad visited him in hospital and it wasn't one of the major hospitals where Europeans went but, horror of horrors, "a Chinese hospital". On arriving there Dad was given the number of the room Phil Godfrey was in and he went down the hall to the room where he found him sitting up in bed, apparently asleep.

All this I heard later when Dad came home looking a bit grim. He hadn't told us the story: my talent for eavesdropping was considerable and I heard the whole gory tale of how he had gone into the room and shaken the bloke in an attempt to wake him. As he was doing this a nurse came by and said, rather matter-of-factly, "He no sleep, he dead."

I can see that bizarre scene playing out in my mind's eye.

As Dad prospered, my parents' nightlife got busier and busier. They were always off to cocktail parties at various embassies or the Australian High Commission, except when they were attending ones held by the Australian Association. It was a very long time since he had renounced his Englishness; Dad was an Aussie now.

Mum was often out to lunch with friends at Gaddi's, the famed French restaurant at The Pen that opened in 1953 and was named after Leo Gaddi, one of the hotel's former general managers.

This Michelin star-winning eatery is still one of Hong Kong's finest and we were treated to dinner there in on a visit in 2017. We were staying at The Pen. When the hotel asked me if we'd like to be their guests for dinner at Gaddi's I leapt at the chance. It's an icon in Hong Kong and that family connection makes it extra special for me. It has a kind of understated opulence, if that's possible, and frankly eating there is like being on a movie set. Its old-world charm I find irresistible and the live jazz band takes requests. I asked them to play *Speak Softly, Love* from *The Godfather* and they obliged, although I think they may have expected us to dance to it. Who did they think they were kidding? Can you even dance to that song? I didn't think so.

Whether at Gaddi's or other Hong Kong restaurants and nightclubs, my parents would often glimpse or run into celebrities. After a night out at the Eagle's Nest in the Hilton on Hong Kong side, they talked about how they had met the British comedian Tony Hancock, who was appearing there. A string of stars appeared at that venue, among them Peter Allen. Mum and Dad had chatted to Hancock after the show and my father remarked on "what a miserable bastard" he was. Tony Hancock was a funny man on stage; in life he had his problems. The year after my parents met him he committed suicide in Sydney which came as no surprise to my father. He had been terribly depressed when they met him and apparently that was pretty obvious.

In the photos I have from those times everyone looks as if they've stepped straight off the set of *The V.I.P.s* starring Liz Taylor and Richard Burton. In their sharp suits and Mary Quant or Chanel dresses, cigarettes in hand, they were all chic-er than chic, and the blokes were all James Bond wannabes. Only one looked like the genuine article. Tony Parr, the … ahem … civil engineer.

I can see him now standing at my father's bar, taking a filter tip out of his gold cigarette case, lighting it and letting out a thin stream of smoke as his tiepin flashes and a wry smile plays on his lips. If he was merely a civil engineer he was a pretty cool one. I still think he was a spy. That's my story and I'm sticking to it.

CHAPTER 16

THE BATTLE OF KOWLOON TONG

Time stood still at the Repulse Bay Hotel. Once you passed through the doors there it was eternally 1932. You half expected a tea dance to start up at any moment.

We used to go there occasionally for a spot of lunch, as they used to say. This grand old hotel by the sea, overlooking a lovely little bay on the southern coast of Hong Kong Island, was one of those hotels like Singapore's Raffles, the Eastern & Oriental in Penang or its sister property, The Peninsula, on Kowloon side – places that exemplified the last days of Empire. The Repulse Bay, which opened on New Year's Day 1920, was built by The Hong Kong Hotel Company, a precursor to Hong Kong and Shanghai Hotels, the Kadoorie family company that established The Pen. My father and his family also frequented the Repulse Bay in the late Thirties, before the shadow of war eclipsed the gracious lifestyle of the Orient.

The guest register here over the years has included everyone from George Bernard Shaw to Marlon Brando and various crowned heads of Europe. Typically, and rather tragically, the hotel was knocked down in 1982. This was one of the greatest acts of vandalism in Hong Kong's history, which is characterised by a litany of such outrages. They built the façade again later, a superficial replica that fronts the apartments now standing there (which are themselves known as The Repulse Bay) as if that could somehow compensate for the sins of the past.

I remember the hotel's cavernous interior and those slowly revolving ceiling fans they used to have throughout the tropics – the sort you see in old films starring men with pencil-thin moustaches, wearing white linen suits and sporting panama hats. I also remember the waiters in their starched white tops. Many of them looked like they had been there since it opened and I wouldn't be surprised if that was the case.

A buffet lunch at the Repulse Bay was one of our occasional Sunday treats. We would prepare for this by a regimen of fasting from the night before. I'm surprised my father didn't attach little 'nil by mouth' tags to our wrists because he was quite adamant that we should starve ourselves ahead of each luncheon taken there. It was the same before we went to yum cha: we needed to have room for the feast ahead.

The Repulse Bay's smorgasbord was sumptuous and my father liked to make several passes of it, piling his plate high and smiling devilishly in the process. If we were all really hungry he figured we would get our money's worth.

Not that money was an issue. During our years living in Kowloon Tong, Dad was a wealthy man. With the colony booming, business was good. Yet he still delighted in bringing home little perfume bottles from planes when he flew first-class and always emptied hotel bathrooms of soaps and shampoos. Keen to capitalise on paying for luncheon at the Repulse Bay by eating enough for three men, he wanted us to do the same. It seemed incongruous considering how affluent he was.

I think it was down to the fact that he had come from working-class stock in South London. Perhaps there were scars from his early years when, abandoned by his parents, he and several siblings were left to sup on bread and dripping when they were supposed to have been looked after by wicked Aunt May.

The only thing he ever said about those early years in London was that he was born near the dog track at Catford. That's it.

Whatever Dad's motivation, he was quite a martinet about keeping us hungry.

The journey to Repulse Bay from Kowloon Tong was much longer in the days before cross-harbour tunnels and the MTR. Dad insisted on driving there himself. On Sundays he gave his driver the day off. Sundays were kind of sacred. Not in the form of religious observance: my parents were never churchgoers. My father's strict Catholic upbringing had something, or everything, to do with that. Sundays were sacred in a secular sense because this was the day my father took time off to spend with his family.

Most Sundays we went for a jaunt. A trip to the Repulse Bay Hotel meant driving to the Kowloon waterfront where we would catch the vehicular ferry to Hong Kong side. Once on board we would all get out of the car – Mum, Dad, my brother and sister and I – and stand by the railings taking in the sea breeze as we chugged through those peculiarly greenish harbour waters. I've never known a stretch of water as opaque. Even in the Sixties it looked almost infectious.

Safety announcements were made in a diffident Cantonese voice through loudspeakers that were much *too* loud. Then they were repeated in broken English and we were always amused because the announcements included a warning that there was to be no "expectorating" on board. Even as the announcement was in progress passengers would be hacking up phlegm and gobbing it over the side in that theatrical manner so beloved of the Cantonese. Mum used to refer to the sounds of Hong Kongers spitting as "the Chinese national anthem". Once, when a man behind her in the cinema was clearing his throat in this manner, she turned around and hit him with her handbag.

On Hong Kong Island we would drive to Repulse Bay over Dragon's Back, that ridge of thickly forested hills which soar behind the concrete jungle. Once across the ridge we would follow the winding roads that skirt the mountains before descending to the bay.

Inside the hotel Dad would drill us in the manner of a military operation, making sure we all filled our plates and went around several times until we were completely stuffed. I would load mine with cold cured meats, bread and coleslaw. No matter how full we were, we could not forgo dessert. He really knew how to enjoy himself, did my old man.

Afterwards we would go for a drive and meander around past the various other bays that are scalloped out of the southern coast of Hong Kong Island facing the South China Sea.

Shek O was another favourite spot. Then, and until quite recently, rich folks who played golf at the exclusive Shek O Country Club had as their caddies women from the Hakka minority. These tiny, tenacious women wore big broad hats with a distinctive black trim. They were rural folk used to hard work but in our eyes the sight of old ladies carrying heavy bags of golf clubs never quite seemed kosher.

The drive from Repulse Bay to Shek O was really a drive in the country and, surprisingly, it's still like that today. The terrain throughout the drive is lush and green, with few houses along the way save for mansions set into the hillsides where people who obviously have way too much money live behind huge iron gates.

Shek O has become a pilgrimage spot for us and each time we visit Hong Kong we make our way there, although no longer by car. We go by MTR and bus and it's still one of the best day trips you can do in the SAR. The journey begins with an MTR ride along the Island line towards Chai Wan in the east which is where the Japanese crossed the harbour during their invasion of Hong Kong in late 1941, some of them apparently swimming across.

We get off at Shau Kei Wan where you surface from the underground station and head for the bus terminus across the road. Here you catch the No. 9 double-decker to Shek O. While doing this you will be harassed by touts working for a mini-bus company which also plies that route. They will try to convince you to ditch your plans and take the mini-bus which they claim is quicker and more comfortable. Pay no heed. They are missing the point entirely.

We have been harangued by these touts many times while waiting for the No. 9. Don't try explaining to these guys why you are taking the bus. You have to ignore them completely. Look straight ahead and do not make eye contact. Eventually they will relent.

Once that's over we board the bus, dribble some coins

into the fare box, climb the stairway to the upper deck, rush forward and grab those front seats because it's from there that you get the full effect of the view.

The bus climbs, deftly navigating the dense concrete jungle of Shau Kei Wan and then, as it grinds gears up the steep road out of town, into view comes the amazing Chai Wan Cemetery, a mixture of amphitheatre and necropolis cascading down the mountainside. Here graves and tombs jostle for the most auspicious positions as decreed by the principles of *feng shui*. At first sight it looks like some residential development spilling down the hill and it kind of is. It's just that all the residents are dead.

It's a steep grade up to Dragon's Back. Trekking the Dragon's Back trail is popular and the trail goes all the way down to the beachside bays of southeast Hong Kong Island, Big Wave Bay and Shek O which, after it crosses the Dragon's Back, winds along narrow mountain roads where cars, trucks and other vehicles almost swipe each other as they pass. There is usually roadwork going on and workmen almost have to dive out of the way every time a bus hurtles past. And hurtle they do because these guys drive like madmen.

The roadside embankments are steep and sometimes concreted at the lower extremities to stop landslides. Concrete aside, this is a verdant world of forests, deep valleys and hillsides that plunge to the sea. Sitting up front you instinctively duck as overhanging branches brush the roof.

For someone who suffers from vertigo I feel pretty brave sitting up there but, vertigo or not, I love what is surely one of the lesser-known treats Hong Kong has to offer.

After navigating the narrow roads of the precipitous central mountain ridges you begin to get the most wonderful sweeping views of the island's south coast which is surprisingly sparsely populated. Dominating the view are those flash houses clinging to the coast and dotted across the water are the pleasure boats of the wealthy.

Soon the bus swings east and Shek O comes into view, seen at first as you would glimpse it from a helicopter – that white crescent of beach, a village hugging the headland, the hillside soaring above it to the west. It is a scene that always elicits a sigh.

Shek O is a wide, sandy beach, not what most people expect to find in Hong Kong. It's set in a lovely little bay flanked at its eastern end by sedate Shek O Village. I like to walk through this village and imagine I might live here one day in one of its cool little tiled cottages. A few Europeans live here along with the local Hong Kongers and that may explain the occasional longboard to be glimpsed leaning against a wall. There are boogie boards too. As you get out to the point beyond the village there is a magnificent walled mansion with views out across the South China Sea.

Clustered behind the beach is a jumble of restaurants and cafés, along with small shops that sell towels and drinks and blow-up rubber rings for kids as well as thongs and snacks. At the western end is a temple dedicated to Tin Hau, the god of fisherfolk. There are some rather mangy dogs around here too. Beyond the temple rises a steep, verdant hill with rocky outcrops. Walk up there to take in the views across this picturesque little bay.

Shek O and nearby Big Wave Bay, the island's premier surf spot, marked the outer extremity of our Sunday drives to

Hong Kong Island. It was one of the last colonial Governor Chris Patten's favourite places and when we visit there now we lunch at the Shek O Chinese and Thai Seafood Restaurant which was his favourite. It's nothing flash, just a jumble of old tables on a concrete floor with a television blaring in the background. They used to have a photo of Patten on the wall there. Not sure if they still do.

And I'm not sure if the Hakka women are still caddying. They do seem to run the beach-umbrella-and-canvas-seat concession, though, and if after arriving you manage to make your way to the beach without getting spotted by them you're doing well.

We usually relent and hire a brolly and a couple of chairs.

It's one of our favourite outings in Hong Kong and whenever we visit I think of our Sunday drives there in the Sixties.

Another patch of coast for regular jaunts was along the shoreline that runs west from Kowloon, past the old San Miguel brewery towards a string of calm, unspectacular beaches where junks used to sail past, turning the scene into a moving postcard. Our regular stop here was a spot called Eleven-and-a-Half-Mile Beach … because it was 11½ miles from the Kowloon-side Star ferry terminal. My father had been coming here since he was a boy.

Sometimes we would venture further along a road that hugged the base of those soaring hills that make Hong Kong's scenery so spectacular. Another of our Sunday lunch destinations was the Castle Peak Hotel, built in 1949 and now – like so much of the architecture from my childhood – gone, leaving only memories behind.

After dutifully fasting all morning we would arrive ravenous. We loved going to the Castle Peak not because it served a fine lunch, which it did, but because they had some of those old arcade machines we loved to play as kids – the ones where you fed in coins and then tried to use the little mechanical hands to grab chocolate bars and little toys from a mound of goodies that mostly seemed too slippery to hold onto.

Lunch itself was excruciating at the Castle Peak, however – to be endured rather than enjoyed, not because of the food, entirely because it involved suffering through a hokey talent quest held there in a misbegotten attempt to keep families entertained. Throughout our meal we were subjected to the most cringeworthy performances by children who couldn't sing or dance and whose poetry recitations had all the charm of a midnight choir of cats fighting on the rooftops.

Awful as this was it was made all the more awful because my father would, time and again, put me forward as a contestant. Looking back, I guess I should be chuffed that he had such confidence in me. OK, I could sing and had recited some poetry at the Hong Kong Schools Music Festival, but I was never going to ruin my Sunday lunch by getting up in front of that audience of muppets.

If I look at photos taken at meals on our outings I'm often looking sour and pouting. I guess I was moody and, as I grew older, less patient with my father and a bit resentful, largely because his drinking was slowly eroding our happy family life in Kowloon Tong. My parents often had rows about that and I think that, being the oldest, I noticed it more than my brother and sister.

If Mum was almost certainly over-protective – apparently

I was a sensitive princeling – my father was always wanting me to toughen up. When he'd put me forward for the talent quest at the Castle Peak Hotel there would be that awkward moment of expectation when the emcee turned his attention to our table and the guests all looked hopefully in our direction to see me sitting there shaking my head, with a face like Mount Rushmore.

So the return journey was often an ordeal, with me sulking in the back and Mum glowering at the old man.

Sometimes we drove in the other direction – out to Clear Water Bay, past the Shaw Brothers studio. The headland overlooking the bay was an idyllic spot, with wonderful views, and we would sometimes picnic there. Between Joss House Bay and Clear Water Bay there's an exclusive country club with, believe it or not, quite a good surf break off the golf links. As a surfer I have been amazed to discover Hong Kong's underground surf scene and in recent years have taken on a few of the breaks. The one off the country club is difficult to access and the club doesn't like surfers hanging around there, according to my friend Simon Chau, co-founder of the Hong Kong Surfing Association. (Yes, there is such a thing.)

As a kid I saw pictures in the *South China Morning Post* of some American servicemen on R&R surfing at Big Wave Bay, and that seemed incredible.

Sometimes, on a Sunday, we would spend the whole day perambulating around the New Territories, that hinterland which makes up around 86 per cent of the former colony. It's called 'New' because it was ceded, by a ninety-nine-year lease, to the British from Qing China in 1898, its territory added to Hong Kong Island and Kowloon peninsula. We would often drive out to Fanling where the Gurkha battalion was based to keep the Communist hordes at bay.

Funny thing about those Communist hordes was that, when you went to the border post of Lo Wu or Lok Ma Chau and looked across into Communist China, you couldn't see anyone. It was just empty rice paddies and fields. The French cartoonist Zabo, who lived in Hong Kong back in the Sixties, drew a very funny sketch showing a crowded border post overflowing with tourists gawking at the bucolic emptiness being pointed out to them as the teeming, overpopulated land of China.

To me it always seemed pretty peaceful – but looks were deceiving.

The New Territories is now pitted with new cities yet there are still swathes of countryside and rural villages. It was a mostly agrarian world in the Sixties and a drive there was basically like travelling back in time.

It was still virtually the old China of the Qing Dynasty, immune behind its border to the ravages of communism and Mao's Cultural Revolution. Life was still lived as it had been in the time of Puyi, the 'Last Emperor'. Clans still ruled the villages and we drove past duck and pig farms with water buffalo standing up to their haunches.

We might stop for lunch somewhere, hungry as always, before heading back to Kowloon Tong. The golf club at Fanling was one of those pit stops. My father occasionally played there.

Sometimes these outings went on for way too long and often I would rather have been at home with my books and stamps and records.

However, rules have their exceptions. One Sunday I was

very grateful to have been whisked away to the New Territories. That drive saved me from being involved in what I have dubbed the Battle of Kowloon Tong.

This was a planned confrontation between a little den of paper tigers and a gang of Chinese boys from the local village and squatters' area. These boys lived in ramshackle abodes abutting ritzy Kowloon Tong and we'd had some run-ins with them, including one shouting match that ended with them throwing bottles at us, bottles that shattered on a concrete path, prompting some local residents to come out and chase us all away.

The leader of our little pack was a friend of mine, Randy Munoz, a tough guy. Randy proved how tough he was by bringing a knife on a YMCA camping trip we'd gone on to some small, rugged islands in the Port Shelter group off Sai Kung in the eastern part of the New Territories. (In all, Hong Kong has 263 islands, which surprises many people.)

We bunked in a big shed there and some of the older boys managed to smuggle in alcohol and cigars. Randy let us practise throwing his knife which we did, sometimes at trees and sometimes between each other's feet, forcing one another into some nimble jumping from side to side to avoid the blade. Eventually the knife was confiscated by Clifton Drury, the benevolent old American missionary in charge of us. He spent a lot of time shaking his head.

At night we had campfires and toasted marshmallows, and – hard as it may be to credit – we all sang that old African-American spiritual *Kumbaya* … although our little group, led by Randy, changed the lyrics to "*Comb my arse, my Lord, comb my arse*".

Randy, who was a proficient smoker, taught me the forbidden art of the drawback in the laneway behind our house in Devon Rd. Before this quantum leap I had only pigeon-puffed. Randy had bought a pack of Lucky Strike cigarettes from the village shop nearby and we lit up away from prying eyes. When I first sucked the smoke down into my lungs it felt like being hit in the chest with a brick.

I coughed and coughed and coughed and, hearing the noise, the old and particularly ornery cook amah from the house next door came out to her back gate and began cursing in Cantonese, then shouted in English: "No smoke! No smoke!" Randy laughed like a drain.

He lived not far from us, in a block of flats on Beacon Hill that overlooked Kowloon Tong. I guess he was an Hispanic-American though we didn't use that description back then. I'd been to his place a few times. The first time, to prove how tough he really was he sculled his favourite tipple, the juice from a jar of dill pickles.

I met his father who wore one of those embroidered Filipino shirts you don't have to tuck in. My dad wore them too. It was the sort of shirt a portly man wore to disguise his girth.

Randy's dad was interested in me because I was an Aussie. I didn't feel like an Aussie. He told me rather proudly that he'd visited Australia and had the kangaroo pelts to prove it. He boasted that he had shot them himself.

I was horrified. To me the kangaroo was a symbol of the homeland I had only a tenuous connection with. It had honestly never occurred to me that anyone would want to kill kangaroos even though I had eaten kangaroo tail soup on Qantas flights home.

Randy's old man didn't have much time for the Chinese, which was a shame given that he was living in Hong Kong. I guess that's where Randy got his attitude from. He wanted to organise a battle with "the Chinks" and I was to be one of his foot soldiers in this war, along with a couple of other members of his little rat pack. Apparently I'd agreed to take part and we met at Kent Road Garden for a strategy meeting, which I attended reluctantly.

Our orders were to get some bamboo broom handles and face down the "Commos".

I wondered how I could get out of this and when it was arranged for the following Sunday I kept my fingers crossed. We didn't go on a Sunday drive every weekend but most weekends Dad had some outing or other in mind. I kept quiet about that, though, and let Randy get on with his plans.

My school week was overshadowed by thoughts of the coming conflict. We were to assemble at Cornwall Street Park then march to the perimeter of the Chinese village and call our foes out.

I had half-heartedly taken possession of a length of bamboo pole Randy had procured for me and propped it round the side of our house.

On the Saturday Randy and I met up at the YMCA in Tsim Sha Tsui where we went to do gymnastics. After the class we had our usual hot dog at the canteen and then I went across to The Peninsula to meet Mum and my brother and sister in the lobby. Soon afterwards Dad arrived and we all headed to the KCC for lunch and a swim.

I usually loved going to the club: now even that had lost its lustre in light of the looming confrontation.

On the way home my father announced the good news: we would be going on a family outing the following day – to Fanling for lunch – and would be away most of the day, which meant I would have to miss Randy's rumble.

Driving back home in the late afternoon I felt a little embarrassed. Still, I was glad to have shirked the showdown. After school the next day we gathered in the park and Randy regaled us with stories about the battle, which I don't think had really come to much in the end. He wasn't overly impressed that I'd missed it. I had established my credentials as a card-carrying coward, which wasn't something I was too concerned about.

I still have a picture of Randy somewhere, in his swimming shorts, standing on a small concrete boat ramp on that small, lush island we camped on with the YMCA all those years ago. A hank of dark hair flops over his forehead and he has a look on his face that seems to say "*Diu ne!*", Cantonese for "Fuck you".

CHAPTER 17

THE MAN FROM HONG KONG

It was the flight from hell that set me up for a life of reluctant air travel. We were on Pan Am flying between Tokyo and Hawaii. My father got good rates on Pan Am because the man who lived next door to us in Kowloon Tong was an executive at the airline, by the name of Cowden. He had sons who were tall and handsome with impossibly white teeth, like the Osmond Family. They were an advertisement for how Americans thought they should be. And Pan Am was a flagship airline, an iconic jet-set carrier with a funky logo although my memories of the now long-defunct airline were forever tainted.

We flew a lot and the leg from Tokyo to Hawaii on a family holiday was supposed to be routine. For my father, at least, it seemed to be. He was always in the air, often by himself on business, but we also travelled extensively as a family from our base in Hong Kong.

Dad was always relaxed about the process – a little too relaxed, if truth be told, especially about boarding. He would often be the last person to join the flight after the final announcement had been made. He would then amble from the airport bar to the gate, quite pleased with himself. Even though I'm a nervous flyer I'm at the airport hours before I need to be, even now, to psyche myself up and get in the zone. I never do quite achieve it, but I try. My old man would not only be late to arrive and to board: when he flew with us he would try to slow down the pace for us as well.

When the announcement came he would tell us there was no hurry. Mum would point out that there was a planeload of people sitting on the tarmac waiting for us. Eventually he would relent and we'd rush aboard, with him bringing up the rear at a strolling gait.

On the Pan Am flight in question he had done his usual trick, had settled himself in his seat, had a quick snifter of Scotch and then fallen into a deep sleep. Within minutes he was snoring. Despite its being a night flight the rest of us were wide awake, my mother gripping the hand rest and staring straight ahead as the plane started bucking. Once we were well and truly airborne we were told the conditions might be a bit bumpy. We were flying through one of those North Pacific winter storms, apparently, the sort that send the swell pumping onto Oahu's North Shore.

That it was a night flight made it worse as far as I was concerned. I like to see outside so I can check that the wings are still attached. I looked at Mum and, as the song goes, '*her face, at first just ghostly, turned a whiter shade of pale*'.

Using her as a barometer wasn't really recommended because her nervousness was infectious. It was already clear I'd inherited her anxious nature. Or had mine just developed in tandem with hers? It was hard to tell. Either way, I was certainly more attuned emotionally to Mum than to Dad.

Mum became incensed because the more she kept calling for the hostesses to find out what was going on the more they ignored her. Turbulence was evidently old hat to them as they sat a few rows behind us chatting to some businessmen, laughing and having a fine old time while we experienced what felt like a roller-coaster ride in mid-air. The old man just snored on, oblivious. This was nothing new.

We regularly travelled home to see family and friends although I must admit I didn't really consider Australia home.

Once, I recall, we turned up back in Hong Kong after a Christmas holiday down under with a suntan to rival American screen actor George Hamilton's. We were stripping off our shirts to form a skins team for soccer at KGV (it was Shirts versus Skins) and everyone else was a bit pasty in the middle of a Hong Kong winter while I was brown as a berry.

"I say, Brown, where did you get that?" the sport master enquired, referring to my tan. "Australia, sir," I answered and he just nodded, before adding: "Jolly good."

We travelled quite a bit around Asia too. A certain incident in Singapore sticks in my memory because it featured our Darwinian relatives (shades of the monkey business that took a bite out of our enjoyment at Pattaya). We had hired a driver to show us the highlights of the island state and he conducted us on a terrifying drive through Singapore Botanic Gardens. As we slowed to a crawl and were taking in the verdant splendour there was a sudden 'thump, thump, thump' on our roof as monkeys jumped out of the trees and onto the car. They peered into the windows hoping we had some food. They seemed to be smiling: at least, their teeth were showing. We were urged not to wind any of the windows down and Mum assured the driver that we didn't need any urging to comply. It was terrifying.

Having been born in 1956, a Monkey year according to the Chinese zodiac, I was often described by Dad as a *maa lau zai*, a term that literally means 'naughty monkey' but is often used to describe mischievous children. I may have been regarded as a monkey yet as you, dear reader, will have sussed out by now I don't have much time for the real McCoy. I like them from afar. There are still monkey populations in Hong Kong – colonies in an ex-colony – found largely around the Kowloon Reservoir but also in Sai Kung Country Park.

Pattaya and Singapore are but two of several scarring encounters I have had with simians. I've run the gauntlet in the Sacred Monkey Forest at Ubud, Bali, where you take your life in your hands. At the Batu Caves just north of Kuala Lumpur fierce monkeys guard the long steps up to the temple. In these places monkeys terrorise visitors and I have run for my life at both locations. In Singapore all those years ago we were safe only because we kept driving.

My father's burgeoning business interests in The Philippines under Marcos (he wasn't yet a dictator but was working on it) meant he was often flying between Manila and Hong Kong. He did consider The Philippines a dangerous place yet eventually agreed to take us along at the invitation of his Filipino business partner, F.F. Cruz.

The highlight of that visit was a journey along a river to the famous Pagsanjan Falls, a day trip from Manila. We went upriver in dugout canoes and I have a photo of me in our canoe with a rather serene Filipina (one of the Cruz clan perhaps?) sitting in front of me just behind the forward oarsman. Behind me all the way was an overweight American woman who looked a bit like the actress Shelley Winters. It was a bit of a joke that I got stuck in the canoe with her because she yapped the whole way up to the falls, seemingly oblivious to the natural beauty all around us, and in the photo you can clearly see her mouth is open.

When we got to the falls we were a little disappointed to find that there – in what we thought would be a pristine remote place – was a small bamboo stand selling soft drinks. I got over my disappointment – and ordered myself a Coke, of course.

Mostly Dad flew 'solo', coming home laden with mini-toiletries from the hotel and plane that he had stashed in his Samsonite briefcase. After greeting him we would gather round to see what goodies he had smuggled and he opened that briefcase like a cross between a magician and a travelling salesman.

Occasionally he would have a story to tell about seeing some celebrity on the plane. The year after we arrived in Hong Kong he had been on a flight back to Hong Kong from Bangkok (this was in June 1964) and when he arrived at Kai Tak said he was surprised to find thousands of screaming girls waiting for him at the airport. Turned out he was on the same flight as The Beatles who had jetted in, *sans* Ringo who was ill. The substitute Beatle was Jimmie Nicol who would go on to play with them in Australia soon afterwards. I never quite got over the fact that my father had been in such close proximity to my idols, or that he came away from that encounter without a single autograph.

Dad was a regular traveller between Bangkok and Hong Kong but we only went there once as a family. We also went to Taiwan for a family holiday in the mid-Sixties. Again, I imagine Dad must have had some business prospects there. He certainly felt sympathetic to Taiwan, seeing it as an example of what China could have been like without the dreaded Communists. According to my recollection, it rained the whole time we were in Taiwan. The highlight of our visit was the national museum which was the repository of the most exquisite Chinese antiquities. Nationalist leader Chiang Kai-shek and his people bought some of China's finest treasures with them when they fled the mainland.

Our family holiday to Japan, which culminated in the flight from hell, was memorable for several good reasons.

We rode the Shinkansen, or bullet train, which had only been running for a couple of years. It was a perfectly blue day as we whizzed past Mount Fuji with a view that was like watching a Hokusai woodblock print in real time.

We spent a few days in Osaka, visited Nara and stopped for another few days at a small hotel near Lake Hakone, including a night in the hotel's traditional wing where we stayed in a *ryokan* and all dressed in traditional Japanese garb, slept on the floor, ate Japanese sweets and drank green tea.

At the hotel I teamed up with another Aussie kid who had discovered a pinball machine in the basement. He'd managed to get it to working without putting coins in it and we spent hours pinging away in boy heaven. Never mind the temples or the exquisite scenery. That free pinball machine still stands out as the highlight.

Being in the mountains and by a lake, Dad thought it might be nice to try a spot of angling. So he asked the hotel concierge to organise a fishing expedition for us. I think he had in mind some romantic notion of us casting for trout in some alpine stream. Instead, we were given a guide who took us to a fish farm. Our pristine mountain stream turned out to be a rather mundane pond where we fished with supplied poles that were merely used to haul our catch out of the water where they could barely swim because they were packed in so tight. It's the first and only time I ever saw fish stand up. You basically threw your line in with a little bit of bait on the hook and immediately dragged a fish out. My brother Steve was so excited at catching such a huge haul that he toppled into the pond at one stage. The odds were stacked in our favour.

We arrived back at the hotel with enough fish to feed the 5000. That evening we feasted on trout for dinner sharing the meal with a young American couple whom my parents had befriended. They were from Dallas, Texas, and their accents were so strong we could hardly understand a word they said. Americans, my mother explained, couldn't talk English properly.

In Tokyo we propped at the Palace Hotel in Marunouchi with an impressive view over the Imperial Palace.

We spent hours watching Japanese television, with European shows dubbed into Japanese, which seemed hilarious to us. After a day trip to Nikko, in the mountains near Tokyo, we flew out to Hawaii on that Pan Am flight described at the start of this chapter.

We spent a few days at Waikiki where my parents bought us matching shirts so that Dad, my brother and I looked like misshapen triplets. Honolulu was a revelation: my clearest memory from that trip is not the soaring mountains, the surf rolling in or the dramatic splendour of Diamond Head: it was seeing people eat ice cream for breakfast. Ice cream and pancakes. That was beyond our ken.

And then we flew down to Sydney.

Our holidays home to Australia all follow a familiar pattern, starting in Sydney where most of our relatives, from both sides of the family, lived. Mum's dad – a Queenslander, and a gentleman of the old school – was a bank manager. He ended up on Sydney's leafy North Shore later in his career and remained in Sydney when he retired. I scarcely knew Mum's mother who, apparently, was difficult and a dipsomaniac, which is what they used to call alcoholics. This was never spoken of but I heard things.

My mother's sister Meg and her husband Maurice, a retired naval officer, lived at West Pymble and they had three children. In addition we had cousins galore – about thirty on the Brown side, one whole family of whom we had never met. My Aunty Eileen, who lived in Yorkshire, had eleven children of whom I've only ever met one – and that's because she migrated to Australia.

We still had a swag of Brown-related cousins in Sydney. My father's brother Bob had five children, and then there was his sister Kathleen who – together with her husband, John Wheeler, mentioned in Chapter 6 – had four children. Aunty Chrissie had three kids but was a little distant from the family. When we returned from Hong Kong on holidays like conquering heroes, the clan would converge on Dixon St. in Sydney's Chinatown, where overeating was the order of the day and the restaurant probably had to hose the tables down afterwards.

After visiting the folks in Sydney we would hire a car and drive to my hometown, Maitland, stopping at the famous reptile park in Gosford. Parked on a stretch of forested road there we would all stay quiet until we heard the magical tinkling call of bellbirds ringing through the bush.

In Maitland we would stay on a farm with my godmother, Jill Scobie. Her husband, Rob, was a dairy farmer whose cows grazed on land the family now uses for growing crops. Their family home nestling in rolling hills at Maitland Vale on the edge of town was a magical sight, a dream world for the likes of us coming from one of the most densely settled cities on the planet. Undoubtedly it nurtured the romantic notions I already had of life in Australia.

A school project I had done back in Hong Kong was about Australian boundary riders. Sitting at the little desk in Kowloon Tong bedroom I dreamt of riding the wide open spaces of the outback. Maitland Vale wasn't exactly the outback but we did get to ride around on horses when we played with the Scobie kids, who to us seemed wild and adventurous. With their father's help they'd built an impressive fort for games of cowboys and Indians and we rode bareback around it attacking its defenders with air rifles and toy bows and arrows.

My father and Rob Scobie would disappear soon after arrival, bound for their favourite pub in the nearby village of Largs, which was named after a Scottish town. They would come back after we were all showered, bathed and in our pyjamas and generally, by that stage, they could hardly stand.

I'm not sure how Rob managed to get up the next morning after those sessions. Dairy farmers have to rise with the birds to milk the cows. Suffice it to say he did.

Our turn at milking would usually come later in the day and I remember picking my way through cow-pats on the way from the car to the dairy where we grappled with teats and the milking apparatus. This was all a huge adventure coming from Hong Kong and being the city slickers we were.

After a few days in Maitland our Australian holiday featured a long drive to the Gold Coast, with an overnight stop on the way – sometimes Kempsey where my father would visit his best buddy from his army days, Jack Lacey, who owned Lacey's Garage in town. To listen to those two you'd come away thinking they'd virtually won the Pacific War between them.

After Kempsey it was north to Surfers Paradise. The Browns had built a bridge near Broadbeach in the late 1950s and had also done the foundation work for a post office in Murwillumbah. While doing that job Dad had stayed just across the border, in Coolangatta, and he liked the Gold Coast.

So it became our ritual to visit there on every family holiday back home, and I for one never suspected that Dad was becoming set on the idea of moving there one day when he was done with Hong Kong.

In Surfers Paradise we stayed at a rather retro old motel, the Riviera Motor Inn, a short walk from the beach. It was run by a fellow we knew only as Thorpie. He had a boat, which was probably his sole justification for wearing a captain's hat. This he 'matched' with Hawaiian shirts and baggy white shorts. His wife was from the Pacific islands, I'm not sure where. She wore colourful dresses and sarongs and, sporting a frangipani behind one ear, looked like something out of a painting by Gauguin.

The motel had a pool for us to frolic in and we spent hours at the beach riding the shore break on Zippy boards – the forerunner of today's bodyboard – and digging in the sand for the tasty molluscs known as pipis. Surfers Paradise then was more of a family destination than it is today. One tourist outing on offer was a day trip with Shangri-La Cruises that included wakeboarding behind the boat which is like a very gentle form of water-skiing. The cruise took us to South Stradbroke Island where we enjoyed a barbecue, eating steaks with our hands.

For all the fun we had it was just a holiday and, while Australia seemed like a playground, Hong Kong was still home. I had no hankering to live in Australia and certainly not on the Gold Coast. Unbeknown to us, Dad had bought land with a view to settling there, Sydney would have been the obvious choice but I think he wanted to distance himself from his somewhat fractious family.

Except for the early years when the Brown brothers all worked for Grandad Bob in Hong Kong, and then in Australia during the Fifties, we have always lived at arm's length from the rest of our kin.

I couldn't wait to get back to Hong Kong, my real home. I mean I knew I *was* Australian, I just didn't feel it. By the time I was ten I felt half English (which I was). The history we studied at school was all English, ditto the literature, and most of the teachers hailed from the British Isles, with the obvious exception of Miss Fung. I spoke with that international British accent that colonial kids in Hong Kong tended to have. When back in Australia I dreamt of Hong Kong and my life there despite all the fun and the endless supply of fish and chips.

Sometimes, even now, when people ask me where I'm from I say Hong Kong, which is, on the one hand, a joke and, on the other, deadly serious.

On one of those long and tedious drives north from Sydney, heading for the sun and a week of getting round in terry towelling, we passed through a little country village. It just whizzed past, we'd barely registered it was a town at all, but it must have been because we heard a siren. The police were following us and my father swore, pulled over and waited for the cops to catch up.

The police car pulled up beside us and a tall policeman with a pot belly sidled up to the driver's window and pulled out a notebook. He scowled at my father.

"You were going pretty fast back there," he said. My father apologised and the cop explained that the speed limit was restricted between the town limits. The old man explained that he hadn't noticed any town limits. He hadn't even noticed a town. That didn't go down well.

"I'm going to have to issue you with a speeding ticket," the cop said, pen poised. Then he asked my father: "Where are you from?"

"Hong Kong," my father replied, and the policeman just gave him a look.

"Don't be funny, mate, where are you from?"

"I'm from Hong Kong," Dad repeated – and, seeing it for the first time from the incredulous policeman's viewpoint, we all started laughing.

CHAPTER 18

THE OLD CURIOSITY SHOP

When I was a boy in Hong Kong several places were off limits and one of these was spoken of only in hushed tones, sometimes overheard at the bar in our home at Kowloon Tong, when I wasn't supposed to be listening to the adults' conversation. That place was Wan Chai.

It was a red-light district and what I knew about that was gleaned from those snatches of conversation I elicited sitting at the bottom of the stairs, unseen, earwigging.

It was, apparently, a "den of iniquity". I'm not sure I understood what that meant. All I knew was that naughty things happened in Wan Chai. It was a rough, tough, seedy place where ladies of the night plied their trade and members of the British garrison went to party and brawl, and to hazard 'having their collars felt' by handcuff-happy Royal Military Police. The famed Scottish battalion the Black Watch was notorious for its Wan Chai antics.

I was too young in the Sixties to really understand much about that – and Wan Chai was never really on my radar, being on the wrong side of the harbour. The wrong side for us, at least. ...

One day on a visit back in 1997, not long before the handover to China, Sandra and I ended up in Wan Chai by default and that incidental detour supplied me with one of the most charming episodes on all my voyages into the culture of Hong Kong. I consider it a tale emblematic of the mystique of the Orient.

We had been shopping in Causeway Bay and wandered westwards, quite inadvertently, into Wan Chai. There we stumbled into a wet market and spent an enjoyable quarter of an hour absorbing all its colour and movement, though by then I was getting a bit green around the gills watching all that live produce slowly expire before my eyes – moribund marine life and raw meat: it was all a bit much no matter how fascinating.

When I stopped in front of one stall to see a fish looking up at me, gills pumping and mouth gaping, I turned to my wife and said, "I think it's trying to say something."

"Yes," said Sandra, "like, 'I'm dying here, help me!' "

We pushed on through the market – me with a moist towelette over my mouth and nose – and into a side street. I guess you could say we were meandering. I've never really been much of a *flâneur*: that day I was. I'm usually pretty ordered in my meanderings, which I know is a contradiction in terms. This day I was indeed a pale imitation of a *flâneur* as I embraced meaningless wandering in one of Hong Kong's most interesting areas.

At that the time Wan Chai was becoming gentrified and now you'll find funky boutique hotels and cafés springing up in that densely populated patch between the harbour and the hills. We stayed there for a few days on one Hong Kong trip long after our first foray there and thoroughly enjoyed it: the proximity to Causeway Bay, shopping heaven, is especially handy. The cathouses and girlie bars are still operating and one night I did see a car full of drunken sailors bent on some sort of mischief pile into a cab out front of the hotel. Good to see some things remain the same.

Things aren't as rowdy now and there isn't as great a need for the houses of ill repute as there was when the British Army was stationed here and the R&R troops from Vietnam escaped the horrors of jungle warfare in the arms of Chinese concubines. I do like that word. It sounds so much classier than 'prostitutes'.

There's a lot to be said for wandering through the streets and lanes of a city without knowing quite where you are or where you are going. We found it refreshing to feel so unfettered.

We called a halt at a small nondescript café and I used my elemental Cantonese to order.

"Bei ngoh leungo ga fey, m'goi." ("Two coffees, thanks.")

Now the sort of coffee you get in these local cafés is a long way from your regular espresso or flat white. We're talking about a black, gooey liquid (like tar, really) in a glass and to that is added a very generous dollop of condensed milk. I love the stuff, Sandra not so much.

"This is the life," I said as I sipped mine and Sandra turned her nose up at hers. Outside I was regarding a streetscape with no other *gweilos* in sight. Being off the beaten track with no tourists in sight always makes you feel superior. It tends to convince you that you are having an authentic experience. That's what can happen to you when you're lost.

After our coffee break we wandered along another street and I could have sworn we were moving in a westerly direction.

We looked around as we strolled. There were Chinese apothecaries with deer antlers and other dried animal bits displayed outside next to Chinese mushrooms and herbs. The smell was, shall we say, impressive. *Ho heung*. Good smell.

There were little grocery and electrical stores and we saw a workman fitting out an old shop spray-welding sparks into the street. No workplace health and safety here! He turned aside to spit as we went past.

We looked in windows, dodged a mangy dog and bypassed men on bicycles mounted with rattan baskets and vegetables. Then we stopped in front of a shop window in which figurines and other curios were displayed behind the murky glass. This immediately caught our interest because we tend to collect such things. The shelves at home are groaning with Buddhas and other booty from our Asian adventures. We even have one made of yak bone that we bought in Kathmandu. At least the teenage boy who sold it to us told us it was yak bone. Yeah, right.

Beyond the grime of this shopfront window we could make out carved ivory, ceramics, jade and other Oriental artefacts that caught our eye and warranted further attention, even though – perhaps even because – the shop seemed like a forgotten remnant of the old Hong Kong, the sort of establishment we used to see on visits to Macau or on Lion Rock Rd, Kowloon, where Mum sometimes took us shopping. Stinky Avenue, she called it.

"Egad, it's The Old Curiosity Shop," I remarked, thinking of Dickens.

"Is it even open?" Sandra said, perhaps to temper my enthusiasm.

"I think it is," I replied, leaning forward into the dark interior. There was no door as such, just a metal grille that had been rolled up not quite all the way. It had either just opened, or perhaps was about to close, it was hard to tell. We went inside, a tad gingerly.

We had to adjust our eyes to the dim interior. The smell was, well, musty to say the least, and there seemed to be a thin layer of dust on most surfaces. It was like walking into an abandoned museum or a mausoleum. It soon became apparent that inside there was – no, not a mummified corpse surrounded by stuff needed in the afterlife – but, rather, a wizened old lady with exaggerated crow's feet crinkling the corners of her eyes. She wore traditional garb – like black pyjamas – and small black slippers. A jade bangle encircled one of her wrists. She half smiled, half bowed as we sidled in and started browsing. If we felt like intruders, she seemed happy enough to see us.

"You have some very interesting things in here," Sandra said, at which she nodded and smiled but it was pretty obvious she did not speak English. Despite the shop's air of decrepitude she did indeed have what looked like some very nice pieces. I looked over a fine ceramic dragon, admired some jade carvings and amulets displayed in a felt-lined tray, and then something else caught my eye. It was sitting behind the fuzzy glass on a low shelf.

A ceramic figurine of a Chinese scholar, a mandarin, blue and white in the traditional manner though the face was glazed a flesh colour, this elegant man was wearing a rather natty hat, pointed at the top. He had a learned look and sported a little Fu Manchu beard. The shining sage held a scroll and emblazoned on the front of the full-length gown that draped over his slippers was a dragon. It was a lovely item. I asked to see it and the little old lady slid back the glass, which wasn't easy for her, and passed it to me. Turning it over in my hands, I inspected the glaze and, well, I'm no expert but it was a pretty solid piece, the sort of thing you see on *Antiques Roadshow* with some expert on chinoiserie going on and on and on about it. Sometimes unexpected items are worth a fortune.

I'm sure I would have been charged a lot for this piece in one of the flash antiques stores up on Hollywood Rd where they follow you down the street pleading with you to buy something if you make the mistake of browsing without purchasing. I asked the price – in Cantonese because I knew how to (*gei doh chin?*) – and the old woman dragged a time-worn abacus out from behind the counter and did some lightning-quick calculations, rattling away on the wooden beads. She then transferred her calculations onto a not quite so ancient battery-powered calculator and came up with a price that equated to around $A30. I looked at Sandra. She nodded.

"I'll take it," I told the little old lady. "*Hai.* Can you wrap?" I made a wrapping gesture.

She nodded, fetched some old newspaper and proceeded to bind it, quite tightly, before tying string around it. Classy. But we weren't done yet. Sandra bought some Buddha beads and we also purchased an oval ceramic vase with courtly scenes painted on the side. This, too, was wrapped in newspaper, and the paper tied with string.

That was enough, we thought, mindful of our already bulging suitcases. Into my backpack they went, and appeared to fit, so I thought I might carry them on the plane back to Brisbane.

Treasures secured, we farewelled the old lady and backed out into the daylight. It was like emerging from a cave. I tapped my backpack, satisfied with the contents and our find – the little old shop that time forgot.

"Bargain," I said. "What a crazy little joint."

"Pretty weird," Sandra said. "We should have bought more."

"There's always next time," I assured her and before the words were out of my mouth I realised that I had cursed myself. So many times have we walked past a shop in Hong Kong and thought *We must come back* – never to find it again.

Shortly after leaving The Old Curiosity Shop behind we stumbled upon another treasure trove – rather a swish store by comparison, dealing in Buddhist devotional items – everything from joss sticks to scrolls, screens and the most exquisite bronze Buddhas.

Things were a little more expensive here but we lashed out and bought a Buddha with a studded cap, its hand in a meaningful gesture that was explained to us and immediately forgotten.

On my bedroom chest of drawers I have a Buddha sitting beside a largish crucifix that came from my grandmother's coffin, a gift to me from a cousin who I guess must have prised it off. I once got a *feng shui* guy around to check our house and he freaked when he saw the Buddha next to the Christian symbol. "No good! No good!" he cried. Apparently the two were incompatible and caused a problem with the house's chi.

Happy with our new Buddha and thrilled with our ceramics, we pledged to return to Wan Chai next time we were in Hong Kong. *Wan Chai isn't so bad after all*, I reflected.

Two years later we did go back searching for our little shop again. We started at the wet market, which I used as a marker. Sandra was convinced we wouldn't find it. Somehow we did, which proved that it hadn't been a sort of mirage. Amazingly the little old lady was still there rustling behind the counter in the gloom, and we went through the same ritual of browsing until I found another lovely ceramic piece … a kind of Chinese Madonna and child, also blue and white. The Madonna was wearing a long cloak decorated with lotus flowers.

As I write the words you are now reading she sits serenely on a shelf in my study, in the company of her scholar friend. Behind them is a photo of my grandparents that was taken in Shanghai sometime in the Thirties. Together they make a singular ensemble, a kind of shrine or altar honouring my family's life in China.

On my desk is an antiquarian print – purchased on the King's Road in Chelsea of all places – a depiction of the old waterfront of Shanghai before it became the Paris of The East.

I am surrounded by talismans and ghosts of the past, and I like it that way.

On our second foray I was tickled to have made another good find and chuffed that we had even found the place again. I was just a bit surprised to find the aged woman still there. She wrapped the Madonna and child in newspaper and tied it with string (of course), and as she did so I wondered if we were her only customers that day, that month … that year?

I'm a creature of habit and the thought gradually took hold that visiting this shop might become our thing, our little touchstone of old Hong Kong. In wistful mood I confided to Sandra the fancy that these visits to that old Wan Chai shop might have been attended by a ghostly apparition that appeared in the temporal form of an old lady. Could she merely be a spirit haunting a shop she used to run? She appeared real enough to us, and the proof is sitting there on my study shelf.

We're frequent visitors to Hong Kong so it wasn't long before we were back and I thought, *Well, third time lucky*. To be back in Wan Chai felt like something out of *Groundhog Day*, replicating the same walk, beginning at the wet market again, grimacing at the sight of fish gasping as they slowly expired in front of shoppers' eyes. Again we stopped for a condensed-milk coffee and strolled on to our little shop, pleased with ourselves.

"Here's the street," I said when we found it again. I suppose I could have marked it down on a map or made some sort of record but it was more fun searching for and rediscovering it this way. We wandered up and down and soon realised we weren't as sure of our location as we'd thought.

"This *was* the street, wasn't it? I checked with Sandra.

"I think so," she said. "Or maybe not." Well, there were two distinct possibilities here after all.

We tried streets parallel to that one – still no luck. Plenty of shops were boarded up, hoardings hid others, so it was hard to tell. A lot of work was going on. I stopped and asked someone – always a mistake because so much is lost in translation. My rudimentary Cantonese merely drew a blank look.

"They know what I'm saying," I said. "They're just messing with my head."

Eventually a man with a face like a full Moon nodded knowingly and pointed frantically to a location down the street. He even walked us part of the way there and seemed pleased when we reached it. It was a 7-Eleven.

"*Ni bin,*" he said. ("*Here.*")

"Oh thank you so much," I said with a little Basil Fawlty sarcasm. We wandered some more but it was clear we weren't going to find it. It obviously wasn't there any more, or so we figured. And the little old lady, if she wasn't a ghost, had almost certainly died.

Maybe we had stumbled on a little portal into the past, a wormhole that contained a dingy little shop for just a little while.

I have no idea if the pieces we bought there are valuable. Should I get an expert to appraise them? I don't want to. I don't need to. As I said, each is a talisman … even though one is a taliswoman. To me they are symbols of Old Cathay; they speak to me of the romance of the Orient, the Orient as I like to imagine it. I look at them; they make me smile. And that's enough.

CHAPTER 19

FAREWELL, FRAGRANT HARBOUR

The Northern Hemisphere summer of 1969 changed everything for me. I know that sounds like the opening of some coming-of-age novel but it happens to be true.

One humid morning I awoke in my bed in Kowloon Tong and had what I think of as 'the sense of an ending', to borrow from Julian Barnes. On opening my eyes I saw the Fab Four looking down on me like a benediction. I had taken the photos of The Beatles from the *White Album* sleeve (that record was just called *The Beatles*, of course, but everyone calls it the *White Album*) and stuck them on one of my cupboard doors.

On the other door, ripped out of a *Fab 208* copy, was a double-page photo of Jimi Hendrix looking the epitome of Sixties 'cool'.

I had spent the first half of 1969 feasting on the *White Album*. I didn't think John, Paul, George and Ringo could top *Sgt. Pepper's Lonely Hearts Club Band.* Now they had done, I immersed myself in the panoply of pop they had created.

On this particular morning The Beatles looked a bit sad too (those portraits aren't exactly happy-smiley) though maybe it was just me. Because I knew we would soon be leaving Hong Kong.

I should have seen this coming. Still, it was a shock. Dad had his land on the Gold Coast, I knew that much. I thought it was just an investment or for some retirement far in the future. For various reasons my parents had decided we would soon be going home. Home. That was the wrong word to use for Australia so far as I was concerned. Hong Kong was home. After nearly seven years it was my whole world.

Life was sweet. I had my friends, my haunts, my stamp collection, my books, my records, and the nice new Jaguar XJ6 in the driveway was used to ferry us to school each day. Life was very good.

I thought again of Richard Hughes's book *Borrowed Place, Borrowed Time*. … but the borrowed time wouldn't run out until 1997 and this was only 1969. For us, that borrowed time had elapsed three decades early. Why? Memories of the reasons we left are hazy. Certainly my brother's health had something to do with it.

He had been ill with some sort of bronchial condition they thought at one stage might be tuberculosis, which was scary. TB and cholera were still extant but it had turned out not to be TB. Still, Hong Kong's worsening smog and humid summers weren't helping.

Another reason remained unspoken. My mother – convinced Hong Kong was the reason Dad drank too much – wanted to start over again in Australia. Admittedly the colonial world and society in which they moved were fuelled by cocktail parties, dinners and drinks at the club and much of my father's business was conducted in an all too convivial fashion. Seriously, though, would doing what they call 'a geographical' help? I guess Mum thought so and Dad went along with it.

Came the moment they told us we were leaving. It was a shock for everyone really. People like our old family retainer, Mr Lai, were devastated. The amah, Ah Lun, looked glum about it too. She had a nice job at 7 Devon Rd with cosy and quite private quarters out the back. Some people were pretty demanding of their servants. I don't think we were that much trouble.

As well as leaving behind Ah Lun; our driver, Jimmy; the gardener; and myriad other support staff, we would also be abandoning our dog, a piebald terrier called Tiny. Months of quarantine in Australia where they were paranoid about exotic diseases wouldn't be fair on Tiny, my parents decided, so we gave him to friends. My father jokingly made them promise not to eat him. He thought that was funny; we didn't. Dog was a popular dish in Sixties Hong Kong. And what of my cat? She was to be given to an Australian lady who had failed to teach me how to play the electric organ.

Our car was coming with us because returning residents were exempt from import tax and all our furniture headed south as well.

I had finished my second year of high school at KGV happily enough and to have it sprung on me that we were leaving, well, I didn't really get a chance to say goodbye to everyone. The new school year would just begin without me and everyone go on as before. They might barely notice my absence.

This was the way of things in Hong Kong. People came from the four corners of the earth and then left, dispersed to the four winds, often never to be heard from again. Nowadays, with Facebook and other social media, I've reconnected with many an old Hong Kong acquaintance and have long been in touch with my close pals Mark Reeve and Greg England, both of whom live in the UK, as well as my Aussie pal Tim Budge, who is in Melbourne. Occasionally I will get an email from someone or a message asking if I am me, that boy from Hong Kong in the Sixties. Yes, it's me, I say and wonder what to say next. "How have you been these past fifty years?" Or something like that.

One of my best friends at KJS was a boy called David Hughes. I think his father was in shipping. He left the colony before us and I kept in touch with him for years. I know he went on to join the merchant marine and got married young but we lost touch and for decades now there has been radio silence, not so much as a trace of him. We were close; our lives diverged; we were lost to each other. Sometimes I think of him and wonder: does he sometimes think of me?

That summer it dawned on me that I would soon be lost to Hong Kong so I was sad, an emotion mixed with a sense of excitement, not to say trepidation. Australia was daunting but we always had fun when we went there. That was a problem in itself, though: fun didn't constitute a life, did it?

So our sentence wasn't to be carried out straight away. There would be a lag that coincided with Hong Kong's long summer break when people go back to their home countries. My father had to wind up his business affairs before we could depart so we spent time in limbo at our compound in the little kingdom of Kowloon Tong, persisting through one last long hot summer.

Our front yard was still a local-area magnet and those friends who hadn't gone on leave congregated there for the usual games and tree climbing. Right up to the bitter end we continued to terrorise the neighbourhood. With some of my pals – partners in juvenile crime – we had taken to egg-bombing the learner drivers who used our quiet streets. As they beetled round in their Morris Minors, we would lurk at the end of the back lanes to ambush them as they passed, unloading our missiles and escaping back down the alleys. We never were caught and my parents knew nothing of this until decades later.

1969 was a tumultuous summer of change. The Summer of Love had come and gone and still the Vietnam War raged on as did the Cultural Revolution across the border, although we were now largely immune to it. This was the summer when John Lennon was considering leaving The Beatles. In September 1969 he would tell the other band members privately that he was leaving and in April the following year Paul would announce publicly that he was leaving and the Fab Four would be neither fab nor four any more.

Our time in Hong Kong coincided almost exactly with their rise, their reign and their fall and, being a Jungian from way back, I see a certain synchronicity in this fact.

It was also during this summer that the Americans put their men on the Moon and in July 1969, as we waited for our Hong Kong end to come, we watched that unfold in grainy black and white on the TV in the corner of our lounge room, running in and out from the front yard all day, sweating in the humidity and then watching in wonder as Neil Armstrong took his giant leap for mankind.

In my room that summer I played the *White Album* endlessly and my new single, *The Ballad of John and Yoko*. I rearranged my stamp albums and continued listening to The Goons at night on my little transistor radio as I waited for the inevitable. Our departure. Which is actually lost to me. I simply cannot remember leaving. Perhaps it was inconsequential in the end, a whimper instead of a bang, or perhaps it was so traumatic that I've wiped it from my memory altogether.

I can recall that long hot summer and then, somehow, it was over and we were back in Australia. It felt to me the way I imagined landing on the lunar surface must have felt to Armstrong and Buzz Aldrin. Australia was an alien land – a big bright alien land that was supposed to be our brave new world – and, so I was assured, our home. On the Gold Coast of all places.

My father had engaged a local architect to design that home, to be built on land – distinctly rural at the time – that he had bought at Cypress Gardens, a few kilometres inland from Broadbeach. Our front boundary was the Nerang River; next door was a farm.

This was to be our dream house, a modern Australian home with some Oriental touches, such as a green tiled roof, a nod to traditional Chinese architecture.

Building it would take time and while waiting we were to rent a house on the Isle of Capri at Surfers Paradise, a place with an ambitious name yet, naturally, nothing like the original Isle of Capri. The house was being built in Amalfi Drive and, again, the locality contained nothing even vaguely suggestive of the Amalfi Coast.

The new abode on our antipodean Isle of Capri wasn't

going to be available immediately so we spent our first couple of weeks back at our old holiday digs, the Riviera Motor Inn beside the Gold Coast Highway on the southern outskirts of Surfers Paradise.

Thorpie was still in charge and still wearing his captain's hat but looked older and a little sadder than he did last time we'd holidayed there. His rather exotic wife was nowhere to be seen. I gleaned from overhearing my parents' conversations that she had run off with a travelling salesman, leaving old Thorpie bereft.

Our first day there was a surprisingly grey one for the Gold Coast where it's supposed to be always sunny. Years later I worked for the local radio station 4GG where they had a rule that if it was raining you were not to mention it on air because that could be bad for business.

I wandered up to the beach, sat in the dunes and watched surfers carve through the glassy, gentle surf under leaden skies.

I was anxious because soon I'd be starting at a new school although initially there had been some confusion about which one. I had been enrolled at The Southport School, an elite boys' school – the sort of place rich folks and the squattocracy sent their sons – but my parents didn't want me to board. The school, however, said it only had room for boarders, something to do with a quota. I may have dodged a bullet there because the school itself majored in rugby and military cadets and I doubt those preoccupations would have suited my temperament.

Instead, my parents decided to enrol me at Miami State High School. My brother and sister would attend Surfers Paradise State School. My sister soon followed me to Miami High and my brother eventually ended up there, too, after a detour via Broadbeach State School. (My sister is the only one who still lives on the Gold Coast as do her daughters, my nieces Kristel and Louise.)

I didn't know anything about Miami High and wasn't aware that it was already developing a reputation as a tough surfie school with a drug problem. Compared to KGV it was on another planet.

First I had to get a uniform and the school checklist stipulated that a hat must be worn so I got a drab grey one that complemented a drab grey rig of shorts and long socks and a shirt too big for me. The hat in particular, I thought, made me look a fool: confirmation of my impression wasn't long in coming.

My first day at Miami High involved Mum depositing me outside the principal's office. She wanted to stay and see me to class but, after assurances from the staff that I would be fine, she left me there, stranded on the veranda outside the head's office, a forlorn figure in my lacklustre uniform and hat. Girls walking past looked at me and giggled; the boys laughed outright.

"Nice hat, dickhead," one of them called out by way of salutation.

Although *officially* a hat was part of the uniform, no self-respecting bloke would be seen dead in one, apparently. In that instant it was made clear to me what a goose I was for wearing one.

I took it off while being escorted to a classroom that seemed to be half full of adolescent boys with long blond hair. Surf rats. Everyone looked at me as if I were a Martian and the teacher, Mr Piccolo – a rotund fellow who also dressed in shorts and long socks and looked like a big kid – introduced me as being from Hong Kong and that sent a murmur through the ranks. Someone behind me said, “Ching chong, Chinaman” and my heart sank.

I felt like a museum or zoo specimen and quietly cursed my parents. *Why had they done this to me?* I was happy in Hong Kong and loved KGV; I was doing well there and had lots of friends and now I was here in this … this correctional facility.

When the bell rang for morning recess I was mortified. *What would I do? Where would I go?*

I knew no one and was too afraid to speak lest my plummy accent should lead to ridicule. So I went and sat on a bench in the quadrangle outside the classroom. My mouth was dry with fear and embarrassment, my tongue stuck to my palate.

Eventually a couple of boys came over. I thought at first that they might want to strike up a friendship, which would have been nice. Instead they seemed to regard me as a sideshow freak that warranted checking out.

“Are you really from Hong Kong?’” one of them asked. I nodded.

“Fair dinkum?” said the other. I had no idea what that meant.

“You’re from Hong Kong,” the boy who seemed to be in charge added, evidently confirming it to himself.

They both pondered this for a few seconds until puzzlement gave way to disbelief.

“You don’t fuckin’ look Chinese,” he declared; and they walked away disgusted. I have never felt so alone.

CHAPTER 20

THERE GOES THE NEIGHBOURHOOD

We stood together, father and son, on a path in Kent Road Garden, Kowloon Tong, surveying this pocket-handkerchief remnant, a modest patch of colonial order. It wasn't exactly the Garden of Eden but for me it was close.

Hamish looked around unimpressed while the sweat beaded on our brows, as if to suggest it had hardly been worth the trek from downtown Tsim Sha Tsui where we were staying, yet again, in the cool confines of The Peninsula.

"Bruce Lee lived here," I said, trying to make it sound more interesting than it probably was. "Well, a few streets south, actually."

That house, Crane's Nest, was in Cumberland Road not very far from where we were standing. I had told Hamish about the theory behind his death that Chinese martial arts masters had him assassinated for revealing the secrets of their mystical arts to the West. The theory concludes that he was killed using the ancient technique of *dim mak* which involves a slight yet deadly touch that sets up vibrations in the body of lethal power. Like me, my son likes a good conspiracy theory.

"You must be shapeless, formless, like water," I said with a certain gravitas. "When you pour water in a cup, it becomes the cup. When you pour water in a bottle, it becomes the bottle. When you pour water in a teapot, it becomes the teapot. Water can drip and it can crash. Become like water, my friend."

"What are you talking about?" Sandra said.

"Bruce Lee, *Enter the Dragon*." Hamish smiled knowingly. We had recently watched that film together.

Rather than stand sweating in this colonial park we would have been far more comfortable in the nearby mega-mall, Festival Walk, which is probably the reason most people come to Kowloon Tong nowadays if they don't live there.

Festival Walk is a sprawling retail paradise. The air conditioning is Arctic in true Hong Kong fashion … so chilly, in fact, that they have an ice rink. When Hamish was small we were tempted to go for a family spin on the ice until the sight of a child being carried off, blood pouring from a gash to his leg from a rogue blade, put us off.

You can travel to Festival Walk and back on the MTR from Tsim Sha Tsui without ever seeing daylight or feeling the heat of the day, an attractive proposition in the steamier months. In that season Hong Kong is a byword for humidity. Water droplets used to form on the inside walls of our home in Kowloon Tong in the days before the whole world was air-conditioned. Our bedrooms had boxy old air-cons: fans struggled to cool the rest of the house.

A typhoon had been brewing in the days before our jaunt to Kent Road Garden. We had spent a couple of days in Macau beforehand and arrived at the jetfoil terminal there to see a sign saying 'Typhoon Signal No. 3 is hoisted.' Not what you want to see when you're about to go on the water. We had a hair-raising ride back to Hong Kong, the boat rocking madly in the stretch of water before the shelter of Lantau Island shielded us from choppy open seas. I couldn't believe that they tried to serve us a meal in the middle of that journey with the jetfoil bucking like a rodeo ride. Gripping my seat, face white as a sheet, I shook my head as they approached with the food.

"Take it away," I shouted.

And so we stood in the Kent Road Garden, baking on this late June morning, as the typhoon now happily made its way towards Hainan, leaving Hong Kong behind, having dodged a bullet this time. Like everyone else we had travelled to Kowloon Tong by MTR on this pilgrimage to my old suburb, to take a look at our old house at 7 Devon Rd. I've done this many times over the years although the house became obscured as part of a larger building that has filled out the block. At one stage a publishing business took it over and, though the gates were still there then, the extension now filled up the front yard where we used to play.

Kowloon Tong, too, had changed but not completely beyond recognition. On our 2016 visit I felt fortunate and grateful to see Kent Road Garden still in existence. I guess it might have been hard for Sandra and Hamish to get a take on what made Kent Road Garden so special to me. It was a lasting memory from childhood, a little corner of old Kowloon that has steadfastly remained the same in an urban landscape fast-changing that it takes a certain effort of the imagination to evoke bygone days.

We strolled up and down the well-ordered path, admiring the topiary, and took note of the graffiti-like scrawl on the wall nearby that said COMMUNIST. Nothing else, just COMMUNIST.

Looking down from Kent Road Garden I could see the railway line, another great survivor. In the 1960s that line was a reminder of the Red Peril because it went all the way to Canton, now known as Guangzhou – a forbidden city in the terrifying land across the border.

The line runs close by the Kent Road Garden and used to look so peaceful. When the train ran by it seemed harmless enough. Sometimes we scrambled down there and lingered by the track, sometimes putting our ears to it – if it wasn't too hot – to gauge if a train was coming.

When it did rattle past, as a kind of protest gesture we would hurl at it stones we had gathered. We deemed that sort of vandalism acceptable because it was our way of railing against the Red Peril (pun intended).

I wondered whether Bruce Lee had ever lingered on the path here in Kent Road Garden. Maybe he did some kung fu moves under the trees in the cool of a Kowloon Tong evening? It was certainly a popular spot for t'ai chi, one of those Eastern exercises we couldn't hope to comprehend. We were both bemused and amused by these people who would turn up in their pyjamas and move slowly, in full public view, to some unheard music as they grasped invisible birds' tails with outstretched hands. They seemed collectively lost in a mystical world invisible to us mere mortals.

We should have respected that. Instead we would hide behind the nearby bushes and taunt them. We were always amazed that they remained unperturbed and just kept slowly going through the motions as if *we* were invisible.

When eventually we graduated to throwing twigs in a desperate attempt to break their trance they just kept on moving, waving their arms like slow human windmills, and in the end we would give up and move on to some fresh delinquency.

Every afternoon after school I would get home, don my blue-and-white rubber-soled sneakers and go out to play and make mischief in one of several local reserves, often Cornwall Street Park just around the corner from our house. A small shop on one corner of the park was run by a Chinese family who lived in a nearby squatters' district.

This family often left their grandma to look after the store – a mistake we ruthlessly exploited. A few of us would go in there and while one kept her busy the others would pinch lollies from the shelves and stuff them into their pockets before running off.

We played cricket and softball in the park. Kent Road Garden wasn't big enough for that sort of thing. We went to Kent Road mostly to ogle the Chinese schoolgirls who congregated there of an afternoon. A shop in the park sold drinks and ice blocks – popsies, we called them then (short for popsicles). We would grab a popsy or a bottle of Coke or Green Spot, and linger there watching as gaggles of girls, in cute little sailor uniforms, sipped their soy milk nearby. The thought of that made us gag. I had tried soy milk once and the taste was so foreign I spat it out immediately. It was a Chinese drink, not for us.

I often came here with my friends to watch these Chinese girls, who seemed ethereal to me. We would sit on a bench and ogle them quite blatantly, as we sipped our drinks or lurked under a tree or behind the topiary. Sometimes they would notice us, giggle and say things behind their hands.

To me they seemed almost courtly, like the mother-of-pearl figures on the lacquer screen displayed in our living room. A poem I wrote many years later, *The Chinese Princess,* was inspired by my memory of our furtive juvenilia, unsure of quite why they moved me as much as they did. It was erotic in a way, though I had no real idea why.

On the day of our family pilgrimage to this storied place we were the only souls in Kent Road Garden. If you can find anywhere in Hong Kong to be by yourself, you're lucky.

It was much smaller than I recalled, and the air was too humid to linger long. Sandra and Hamish yearned to head back to the hotel for a swim. I insisted we walk around to Devon Rd – a short stroll from there – to complete the pilgrimage.

En route we passed a house that had once been home to two teachers from KJS, one of whom was Australian. They had been busted for marijuana possession (well, it was the Sixties) and swiftly deported. That was quite a scandal.

Swinging right from Cornwall St. into Devon Rd, our house was just a couple down from the corner. The house next door to ours had been replaced by a vast Italianate mansion with a Bentley in the driveway.

I was shocked to find that where the iron gates once stood, marking the entrance to our driveway, now there was just some hoarding. I found a gap and peered through, the sweat on my brow dripping onto my glasses.

The shock deepened.

Our house was gone!

In the space it had stood there was only a cleared site where another monstrosity like the one next door would no doubt arise before long.

"Can you believe that? They've knocked it down," I said.

"Does that surprise you?" Sandra countered.

Even though the façade of our old house hadn't been visible for years I felt comforted by the fact that it had survived, if only in Potemkin form.

It seemed like sacrilege that it had been obliterated. I was devastated. For me that house was a symbol of everything grand and wonderful about our life in Hong Kong. In an era of uncertainty it had been the one constant. We felt safe there even at the peak of the riots in 1967 when the Cultural Revolution spilled onto the streets of Kowloon.

Reason told me it couldn't have stayed as it was – the land was just too valuable – but my heart seldom listens to my head.

Away we walked down Devon Rd and around the corner back towards Kowloon Tong station. I decided to catch a taxi downtown, though, rather than fight the crowds on the MTR. There was a rank outside the station so we jumped into a taxi and sighed with relief on finding the interior suitably frigid.

"Tsim Sha Tsui," I told the driver and he just looked at me. "Tsim Sha Tsui,"

I repeated. "Peninsula Hotel, OK?"

He shook his head to signify he hadn't a clue what I was talking about. I reckoned he was having a lend of me yet couldn't be certain his ignorance was feigned.

"Right," I declared, flinging the door open and getting out. Sandra and Hamish followed.

"Let's try this one," I said, flustered. Opening the door, I said to the driver, "Tsim Sha Tsui?" and he, too, shook his head. It was hot as Hades and I was determined to have a nice cool cab ride back to our hotel. These guys obviously didn't want to take *gweilos*.

"One more," I said and opened the door of the next cab. The saying 'third time lucky' may have crossed my mind. A few amused passers-by had now stopped to watch the free entertainment.

"Tsim Sha Tsui? Peninsula Hotel?" I said and this driver nodded. "Thank Christ for that," I said.

We flung ourselves into the cab and sped off. Soon we were on Waterloo Rd heading downtown. I sat back and pictured our house, framed by trees, fringed with bamboo; and those big, blue iron gates and the compound wall that had kept the world at bay.

"I can't believe it's gone," I said – and now I was the one shaking his head.

Later, I sat, as I often do in The Pen's Harbour View rooms, surveying the action on the water. It's like watching a postcard come to life as the Star ferries track back and forth. And over there, far below, was the *Duk Ling* bobbing like a cork near the Kowloon waterfront.

I was still fixated on the loss of our old house. That must have taken a bit of work: it was pretty damned solid. Gone from the physical world, it still existed in my heart and mind.

I can close my eyes now and walk through it in the cool of the afternoon, can see and hear the trees swaying in the breeze. I can walk out onto the front terrace, look up and see Lion Rock crouching there, a friendly guardian presiding over the little faraway realm of Kowloon Tong.

I closed my eyes then and drifted back to that lost world

where ghosts from my past flickered like images in some grainy home movie. Soon the lights of Hong Kong Island started to come on as dusk descended on the Fragrant Harbour.

ACKNOWLEDGEMENTS

Thanks to my publisher, Barry Scott, for being interested in my tale of Hong Kong and giving me the opportunity to share it. And many thanks to my editor, Ken Haley, who is the personification of the word 'meticulous'.

Thanks to my wife, Sandra McLean, and son, Hamish Brown, for listening to my Hong Kong stories. I am so glad they love the place as much as I do. Madonna Duffy helped me get the ball rolling and I appreciate her support and friendship. Thanks to Ross Fitzgerald who remained steadfast in his belief in this book, and to Craig Munro for advice early in the piece. Also cheers to Manfred Jurgensen for always supporting my writing. Thanks also to Sian Griffiths, former PR whiz for The Peninsula Hotels chain, for rekindling our love for The Peninsula Hong Kong and helping us reacquaint ourselves with it. Thanks to The Peninsula Hong Kong for exemplary service and hospitality, as well as to The Mint Partners who look after public relations in Australia for The Peninsula Hotels chain. Also to the Hong Kong Tourism Board for assistance over the years, and to the Kowloon Cricket Club. Thanks also to my first reader, Amanda Weaver.

Prototypes of some chapters have appeared in *Griffith Review* (*Hong Kong 1967: Summer of Discontent*, GR 18, Summer 2007-2008) and *StylusLit* (*The Battle of Kowloon Tong*, Issue 1, 2017; *Remember the Sidetracks*, Issue 2, 2017).

I am indebted to the following publications: *Tales of Old Hong Kong* by Derek Sandhaus (Earnshaw Books, 2010);

Borrowed Place, Borrowed Time: Hong Kong and Its Many Faces by Richard Hughes (André Deutsch, 1968); *Hong Kong* by Jan Morris (Vintage Departures/Vintage Books, 1988); *A Concise History of Hong Kong* by John M. Carroll (Hong Kong University Press, 2007); *Hong Kong, 1997* by David Bonavia (A *South China Morning Post* publication, 1985); *Chasing Rickshaws* by Tony Wheeler and Richard I'Anson (Lonely Planet, 1998); *The Peninsula Hong Kong* by Andreas Augustin, part of The Most Famous Hotels of the World series (Treasury Publishing, 1991); *The Skeptical Romancer, Selected Travel Writing* by W. Somerset Maugham, edited by Pico Iyer (Everyman's Library, 2009); and *Michael: My Brother, Lost Boy of INXS* by Tina Hutchence with Jen Jewel Brown (Allen & Unwin, 2018).

Thanks to Hong Kong friends including Greg England, Tim Budge, Mark Reeve, Judy Seaton, David McKirdy (whose extensive knowledge about all things Hong Kong was invaluable), Simon Chau, Liam Fitzpatrick and James Hall. And to my sister, Jane, and brother, Steve, who lived the dream with me.

Phil Brown is Arts Editor of *The Courier-Mail* and has a popular column in the lifestyle magazine *Brisbane News*. He has written for a range of national and international newspapers and magazines and has published his poetry widely in the mainstream press and literary journals. He is the author of two books of verse - *Plastic Parables* (Metro Community Press) and *An Accident in the Evening* (Interactive Press). His book of humorous travel stories, *Travels with My Angst* (UQP, 2004) was short-listed for the Arts Queensland Steele Rudd Award at the 2005 Queensland Premier's Literary Awards. *Any Guru Will Do* (UQP 2006) was the second in his memoir series. From 1963 to 1970 he lived in Hong Kong where his father ran a construction company. He lives in Brisbane's north with his wife Sandra McLean, son Hamish and a Maltese Shi Tzu called Sarge.